MEN WHO MET GOD

MEN WHO MET GOD

A·W·TOZER

COMPILED AND EDITED BY
GERALD B. SMITH

CHRISTIAN PUBLICATIONS
Camp Hill, Pennsylvania

Christian Publications
3825 Hartzdale Drive, Camp Hill, PA 17011

The mark of ✝ vibrant faith

ISBN: 0-87509-377-9
LOC Catalog Card Number: 86-70773
© 1986 by Christian Publications
Printed in the United States of America

CONTENTS

INTRODUCTION

For a quarter of a century, it was my great privilege to know Aiden Wilson Tozer well. Our paths crossed at Bible conferences and at denominational meetings. I preached in his church. I was in his home.

Almost without fail, whenever we met, we prayed together. In those sacred moments the presence of God was very real as Tozer talked *to* the One *about* whom he preached and wrote.

When in 1953 Tozer suffered a heart attack, he accepted an invitation from my wife and me to convalesce in our Florida parsonage. During those weeks, my wife and I looked after him. With him I read galleys of his book, *The Knowledge of the Holy*.

Tozer was a great preacher, widely sought after. He addressed some of North America's largest religious gatherings. But acclaim never turned him from the simplicity and genuineness he learned as a boy on the farm in his "beloved Pennsylvania."

Largely self-taught, he knew language like few others. He was a precise craftsman in its use. But those who pressed to hear him preach, including great numbers of college and university students, found in A. W. Tozer more than a master wordsmith. They saw in him a man to whom the knowledge of God and Christian experience were supreme realities.

The spirituality Tozer enjoined was always wholesome, positive, biblical. There were flashes of wit in his preaching, and there was refreshing humor. Invariably, people were challenged to know God better. They went away with hearts warmed and minds renewed.

The chapters of this book were originally some of the sermons Tozer's congregations listened to so eagerly. Under the skillful hand of Gerald B. Smith, compiler and editor, what once made good hearing now makes good reading.

Men Who Met God is A. W. Tozer at his best. Simple. Genuine. Compelling. Look for mature insight, moral earnestness, unfaltering logic. Be surprised by the sudden jolt of a pointed remark.

This is a book worthy of sharing with spouse, family and friends. It bears reading aloud. One way to grow in God is to nourish your soul with high thoughts about Him. In this book, Aiden Wilson Tozer will show you the way.

Robert W. Battles
Orlando, Florida
1986

"We Preach Christ"

. . . *and we never apologize for true Christian experience*

WE ARE IN tune with the plain teachings of the Bible when we attach great importance to genuine Christian experience. But I will take immediate objection to the charge, "Tozer preaches experience!" I do not preach experience. I preach Christ. That is my calling, and I will always be faithful to that calling.

Nevertheless, I want to shed some light on this matter of experience. I insist that the effective preaching of Jesus Christ, rightly understood, will produce spiritual experience in Christian believers. Moreover, if Christian preaching does *not* produce spiritual experience and maturing in the believer, the preaching is not being faithful to the Christ revealed in the Scriptures!

Let me say it again another way. The Christ of the Bible is not rightly known until there is an experience of Him within the believer, for our Savior and Lord offers Himself to human experience.

When Jesus says, "Come unto me, all ye that labour and are heavy laden," it is an invitation to a spiritual experience. He is saying, "Will you consent to come? Will you make this a journey for your heart, not your feet? Have you added determination to your consent? Then come. Come now!"

Jesus Christ, truly known and loved and followed, becomes a spiritual experience for seeking men and women. That, in essence, is the thesis of this book.

As a boy, I was not a Christian. I did not have the privilege of growing up in a home where Christ was known, loved and honored.

God spoke to me through a street preacher as he read Jesus' words I already quoted from Matthew 11:28: "Come unto me, all ye that labour and are heavy laden, and I will give you rest."

That invitation let me know that Jesus is still saying, "Come. Come now!" I went home and up into the attic, where I would be undisturbed. There in earnest prayer I gave my heart and life to Jesus Christ. I have been a Christian ever since.

My feet took me home and into the attic. But it was not my feet that went to Jesus. It was my heart. Within my heart I consented to go to Jesus. I made the determination, and I went!

I am positive about the validity, the reality and the value of Christian experience. Jesus is a person and He has all the attributes of personality. We can talk to Him just as we talk to our other friends. He says, "Come to me and tell me all your troubles." You can tell Him anything. You can say anything to the Lord Jesus you want to say.

If you find His way hard, tell Him so. He does not get angry, and He does not turn away from you. Why should we not tell Him everything? He already knows everything about us!

Yes, our Lord gives Himself to us in experience. David says, "O taste and see that the Lord is good" (Psalm 34:8). Either that is a wild figure of speech that must be discarded as visionary, or it means something. I think it means something.

I believe the Holy Spirit was saying through David, "You have taste buds in your soul for tasting, for experiencing spiritual things. Taste and experience that God is good!"

Our shortcoming in spiritual experience is our tendency to believe without confirmation. God Himself does not need to confirm anything within His being. But we are not God. We are humans, and in matters of our faith we need confirmation within ourselves.

Why are so many Christian believers ineffective, anemic, disappointed, discouraged? I think the answer is that we need confirmation within ourselves and we are not getting it.

I have no doubt that God, in love and grace and mercy, awaits to confirm His presence among those who will truly hunger and thirst after righteousness. For a long while I have been on record insisting that true spiritual experience is conscious awareness, illustrated early in the Old Testament by Abram's personal realization and knowledge of the presence of God.

In the Christian church, genuine spiritual experience goes back to the apostles—actually back to our Lord Himself. I do not refer to a dream while a person sleeps. I do not refer to something a person has buried in his or her subconsciousness. I refer to a conscious intelligence, an awareness.

The human personality has a right to be consciously aware of a meeting with God. There will be a spiritual confirmation, an inward knowledge or witness.

I repeat: Experience is conscious awareness. This kind of confirmation and witness was taught and treasured by the great souls through the ages.

Conscious awareness of the presence of God! I defy any theologian or teacher to take that away from the believing church of Jesus Christ!

But be assured they will try. And I refer not just to the liberal teachers. God has given us the Bible for a reason. That reason is so it can lead us to meet God in Jesus Christ in a clear, sharp encounter that will burn on in our hearts forever and ever!

There are teachers whom I call "textualists" who often put the Bible ahead of God. A textualist is someone who magnifies the Bible text to the disregard of the God who inspired the text. He—or she—holds the Bible in such a way that no one can see the light.

When the Bible has led us to God and we have experienced God in the crisis of encounter, then the Bible has done its first work. That it will continue to do God's work in our Christian lives should be evident.

Yet I have heard some people say only doctrine is important. They would leave no room for Christian experience. But consider the preaching and the example of the famed Jonathan Edwards, used so mightily by God in the Great Awakening throughout New England in the 18th century.

But, you say, Jonathan Edwards was a Calvinist!

I know. And that is my point. Edwards was acknowledged by society to have been one of the greatest intellects of his time and one of the most powerful and successful ministers in history. He wrote a forceful book, *Religious Affections*, which in his day meant religious emotions. Edwards was not a Methodist. He was not a member of the Salvation Army. If he had been either, the fundamentalists of the day would have spiked him with the comment, "Well, he is an Arminian, you know!"

No, Edwards was a Calvinist. But he believed in genuine Christian experience so positively that he wrote his book in defense of Christian emotions. Charged by some that his revivals had too much emotion in them, Edwards stood forth and proclaimed that when men and women meet God, accepting His terms, they experience an awareness that lifts their hearts to rapture.

After all, what higher privilege and experience is granted to mankind on earth than to be admitted into the circle of the friends of God?

Abraham, called in the Bible the father of the faithful, demonstrated in many ways that he had experienced the reality of another and better world. He saw that sphere, that kingdom in which a living God reigns and rules and still encourages men and women to become His friends.

God, being perfect, has capacity for perfect friendship. Man, with his imperfections, can never quite know perfection in anything, least of all in his relationship to the incomprehensible Godhead.

Intellect, self-consciousness, love, goodness, holiness, pity, faithfulness—these and certain other attributes are the points where likeness between God and man may be achieved. It is here that Divine-human friendship is experienced.

It is well for us to remember that Divine-human friendship originated with God. Had God not first said "You are My friends," it would be inexcusably brash for any man to say, "I am a friend of God." But since God claims us for His friends, it is an act of unbelief to deny the offer of such a relationship.

When we consider the reality of this God-mankind relationship, we are considering the truth and reality of genuine Christian experience. Genuine Christian experience must always include an encounter with God Himself.

The spiritual giants of old were those who at some time became acutely conscious of the presence of God. They maintained that consciousness for the rest of their lives.

The first encounter may have been one of terror, as when "an horror of great darkness" fell upon Abraham or as when Moses at the burning bush hid his face because he was afraid to look upon God. But reading on, we learn that this fear soon lost its terror and changed rather to a delightful awe. Finally it leveled off into a reverent sense of complete nearness to God.

The essential point is this: These were men who met and experienced God! How otherwise can the saints and prophets be explained? How otherwise can we account for the amazing power for good they have exercised over countless generations?

Is it not that indeed they had become friends of God? Is it not that they walked in conscious communion with the real Presence and addressed their prayers to God with the artless conviction that they were truly addressing Someone actually there?

Let me say it again, for certainly it is no secret. We

do God more honor in believing what He has said about Himself and coming boldly to His throne of grace than by hiding in a self-conscious humility.

Those unlikely men chosen by our Lord to serve and minister as His closest disciples might well have hesitated to claim friendship with Christ. But Jesus said to them, "Ye are my friends."

The Spirit of God has impelled me to preach and write much about the believer's conscious union with Christ—a union that must be felt and experienced. I will never be through talking about the union of the soul with the Savior, the conscious union of the believer's heart with Jesus.

Remember, I am not talking about a theological union only. I am speaking also of a conscious union, a union that is felt and experienced.

As a preacher and minister of Christ's gospel, I have never been ashamed to tell my congregations that I believe in feelings. I surely believe in what Jonathan Edwards termed religious affections.

That is man's perspective.

I also am aware that from God's perspective there are qualities in the Divine Being that can never be explained by intellect. They can only be known by the heart, the innermost being of man. John said it long ago: "Hereby perceive we the love of God, because he laid down his life for us" (1 John 3:16). So it is best for us to confess that as humans we have difficulty in really understanding what God has said when He says that He loves us.

Do you follow me when I say that love can only be understood by the feeling of it? Think of the warmth of the sun during a summer day. Tell a person in the arctic that it is a warm day and he will not under-

stand what you mean. But take him out in the blaz-
ing rays of an American summer and he will soon
know that it is a warm day! You can know more
about the sun by feeling than you can by description.

For men and women who have met God, we may
say that the sun—the Son—has come up in their
hearts and His warmth and light have given them a
distinguishing radiance. They have the inner witness!

Perhaps you will agree with me when I say sadly
that the average evangelical Christian is without
this radiance. Instead of an inner witness, he or she
too often is found substituting logical conclusions
drawn from Bible texts. There is no witness, no encounter with God, no awareness of inner change.

The whole point that I am making about the fellowship of a person with God is this: where there is
a divine act within the soul, there will be a corre-
sponding awareness. This act of God is its own evi-
dence. It addresses itself directly to the spiritual
consciousness.

It is within this context of awareness and fellowship and communion with God that I would comment on three abiding elements of Christian experience and spiritual life. These are elements that are
always the same among men and women who have
had a personal meeting with God.

First, these great souls always have a compelling
sense of God Himself, of His person and of His
presence. While others would want to spend their
time talking about a variety of things, these godly
men and women, touched by their knowledge of
God, want to talk about Him. They are drawn away

from a variety of mundane topics because of the importance of their spiritual discoveries.

Second, it is plain that the details and the significance of their personal experiences remain sharp and clear with true spiritual meaning.

But a word of caution. I am not referring to any need or formula for identical Christian experiences. We ought to be fully aware that in the body of Christ we are not interested in the production of "cookie-cutter" Christians. It is actually a tragic thing for believers to try to be exactly like each other in their Christian faith and life.

Let me also put in a word here about our Christian testimonies. I have always treasured the humble testimonies of those who have found joyous radiance within their beings because they have met Jesus Christ and know Him as Savior and Lord. I am probably overly cautious about testifying to my own experiences because I do not want anyone to be tempted to try to copy anything the Lord has done for me. God has given each of us an individual temperament and distinct characteristics. Therefore it is the office of the Holy Spirit to work out as He will the details in Christian experience. They will vary with the personality.

Certainly we can be sure of this: whenever a person truly meets God in faith and commitment to the gospel, he will have a consciousness and a sharp awareness of the details of that spiritual transaction.

The third element is the permanent and life-changing nature of a true encounter with God. The experience may have been brief, but the results will be evident in the life of the person touched as long as he or she lives.

To summarize: We can always trust the moving and the leading of the Holy Spirit in our lives and in our experiences. On the other hand, we cannot always trust our human leanings and our fleshly and carnal desires.

I must also add another word of balance. We know that the emotional life is a proper and noble part of a man or woman's total personality. But by its very nature it is of secondary importance. Religion lies in the will and so does righteousness.

God never intended that such a being as mankind should become the mere plaything of his or her feelings. The only good that God recognizes is the willed good. The only valid holiness is a willed holiness. That is why I am always a little suspicious of the overly bubbly Christian who talks too much about himself or herself and not enough about Jesus.

Then, I am always a little worried about the "hope-so" Christian who cannot tell me any of the details of his or her Christian experience.

And, finally, I am more than a little concerned about the professing Christian whose experience does not seem to have resulted in a true inner longing to be more like Jesus every day in thought, word and deed.

"I Will Pay Any Price"

Abraham was on his face, God was on the throne

I HAPPEN TO believe that Abraham's encounters with the living God nearly 4,000 years ago leave modern men and women without excuse.

Abraham stands for every believer. His eager and willing faith becomes every Christian's condemnation. On the other hand, his fellowship with God becomes every believer's encouragement.

If there is a desire in your heart for more of God's blessing in your life, turn your attention to the details of Abraham's encounters with God. You will find yourself back at the center, at the beating heart of living religion.

It is profitable for us to remember that when he was still Abram, living in a segment of the world that we now identify as Syria, humans were completely occupied with a wide variety of gods. Religious expressions were based on many forms of pagan idolatry.

Remember, too, that at that point in history, almost 2,000 years before the coming of Jesus Christ into our world, Abraham had no Bible and no hymnal. He had no church and no godly religious tradi-

19

tions for guidance. He could not turn to a minister or an evangelist for spiritual help.

Abraham had only his own empty, hungry heart. That and the manifestation of the God who reveals Himself to men and women who desire to find Him and know Him!

The Bible informs us that Abraham heard the word of the Lord—an audible communication from a living, eternal Being. It was a revelation that takes us back to the ancient fountain of true worship, back to the roots of a living and meaningful religion. It takes us back to a time before there were churches, denominations and forms of worship—things we now take for granted. But remember, Abraham predated them all.

The Lord God was about to do something special in our sinful world. He needed a man who would believe and trust and obey just because God is God!

Abraham was that man. In the course of his fellowship with God, Abraham heard the Lord say, "I am the Almighty God; walk before me, and be thou perfect. And I will make my covenant between me and thee, and will multiply thee exceedingly. . . . A father of many nations have I made thee" (Genesis 17:1-2, 5).

Abraham had a glorious and continuing experience with the Almighty God. And spiritual experience is as real and valuable yet today as at any time in the history of God's dealing with mankind.

Let me define what I mean by experience. It is conscious awareness. Experience is awareness within a person's conscious intelligence.

Think about the reality of Abraham's experience. Abraham was consciously aware of God, His presence and His revelation. He was aware that the living God had stepped over the threshold into personal encounter with a man who found the desire within himself to know God, to believe God and to live for God.

See the effect of this encounter on Abraham. He was prepared to pay any price for the privilege of knowing God. For certain he recognized the lofty, holy character of the Creator and Revealer God.

The Scriptures declare, "Abram fell on his face" as the Lord talked with him (Genesis 17:3). Abraham was reverent and submissive. Probably there is no better picture anywhere in the Bible of the right place for mankind and the right place for God. God was on His throne speaking, and Abraham was on his face listening!

Where God and man are in relationship, this must be the ideal. God must be the communicator, and man must be in the listening, obeying attitude. If men and women are not willing to assume this listening attitude, there will be no meeting with God in living, personal experience.

This probably explains why there are so many shallow, empty Christian believers in our day—dissatisfied men and women in our churches who exhibit little delight in the things of God. To them, Christianity is a rather humdrum, monotonous religious practice. They seem never to have been gripped within by the world's most tremendous and awesome experience—an encounter with the majestic God whose being fills His universe.

Yes, Abraham was lying face down in humility and reverence, overcome with awe in this encounter with God. He knew that he was surrounded by the world's greatest mystery. The presence of this One who fills all things was pressing in upon him, rising above him, defeating him, taking away his natural self-confidence. God was overwhelming him and yet inviting and calling him, pleading with him and promising him a great future as a friend of God!

This is God's way and God's plan. This is God!

As we examine the nature of believing faith in our day, we find ourselves asking, "Where is the mystery? Where is the reverence, the awe, the true fear of God among us?"

As humans we are prone to reduce our concept and estimate of God. We are to the point where we presume we can manage and maneuver Him—perhaps even push Him around on occasion.

How wrong can we be?

The great God and Father of our Lord Jesus Christ rises beyond our consciousnesses, rises above our abilities and our questions. His infinitude is known only to Himself, the One who created and who is able to redeem and forgive.

This is the God who drew near to Abraham. This is the God who later approached mankind in mankind's own flesh, who was called Immanuel—God with us. No wonder Abraham was stretched out, on his face, before that Presence!

God was saying, "Abraham, I am trying to tell you something—something very important. I want you to listen and to comprehend. Abraham, you were made in My image and you were designed for a single purpose: to worship and glorify Me."

We are surrounded throughout our lifetime by a multitude of things designed for specific purposes.

Without argument, most things are at their best when they are fulfilling their purpose and design.

For instance, a piano is made with a specific purpose: to produce music. However, I happen to know that someone once stood on a piano in order to put a fastener of some kind in the ceiling. Some artistic women have used piano tops as family picture galleries. I have seen piano tops that were cluttered filing cabinets or wide library shelves.

There is an intelligent design in the creation of a piano. The manufacturer did not announce: "This is a good piano. It has at least 19 uses!" No, the designer had only one thought in mind: "This piano will have the purpose and potential of sounding forth beautiful music!"

Or consider the design of our ears. They are at their best when they serve our hearing as God intended when He made us. But some people seem to think that God designed ears just to hold glasses in place.

Do not miss the application of truth here. God was saying to Abraham, "You may have some other idea about the design and purpose for your life, but you are wrong! You were created in My image to worship Me and to glorify Me. If you do not honor this purpose, your life will degenerate into shallow, selfish, humanistic pursuits.

"Abraham, commit your whole life and future into My hands. Let Me as your Creator and God fulfill in you My perfect design. It is My great desire that you become a faithful and delighted worshiper at My throne."

My Christian brother or sister, you who follow the Lamb, you do not need me to tell you that our faithful God has a master design for each life. God has a master design for *your* life.

God knew that Abraham was a man, a human, and that he belonged to a fallen race. Yet God's word to Abraham was not a condemning word. It was an encouraging, a supportive word. So it is with God's word to us, even in our day. He still asks, "Are you willing to worship Me and glorify Me?"

We were so designed and created. We were made in the image of God. And God is prepared to receive us and welcome us through His love and goodness as though we had never been the sons and daughters of misery and darkness.

As followers of the Lamb, we know this wonder and this miracle. Our way into fellowship and friendship with the God of all creation is by the blood of the everlasting covenant, Jesus Christ Himself being our sacrifice, our redemption and our surety.

I see a beautiful and engrossing lesson in these experiences of Abraham. It is a lesson as real in this century as in Abraham's time. God by His very being and nature had been there all the time, but Abraham had just become acquainted with Him in wondrous, personal encounter!

This has been true of all the great saints, no matter when or where they lived. We have the biographies of many of them. Others lived, encountered God and served in their own time and sphere with little notice but with God's blessing.

I have had the opportunity to write about three spiritual giants in my own generation. The three were Albert B. Simpson, the Presbyterian divine who founded The Christian and Missionary Alliance; Robert A. Jaffray of the Toronto Globe family, the missionary genius who found ways to take Christ into many forbidden areas of Asia and the Pacific Islands; and humble lay evangelist Tom Hare, known personally to many of us as "the Irish plumber."

The three were alike in the sense that all had met God very definitely in personal encounters and ever after could say in wonder, "God was faithful—and He had been there all the time!" Each had a burning, personal experience with our Lord.

In terms of culture, education and methods of ministry, they were as unlike and different as three men could be. But God had said the same thing to each of them, the same thing He had said to Abraham: "When you have found Me, your Creator, your Redeemer and your Lord, you have found everything you need! It will be your privilege to trust and obey. It will be My privilege to bless you, guide you and sustain you!"

They were three of those who in this era found their great example of faith in Abraham. If we had the names and the experiences of all the saintly men and women who encountered God throughout the centuries, we could fill many great libraries.

Some of them we would consider great, but many of them were very ordinary people. Some were rich, but many more were poor. Some were highborn, but many of the lowborn were God's true royalty in the society of mankind. Some of them were kings and leaders, but God's final records are going to reveal shining crowns and eternal rewards for saintly scrubwomen, tradespeople and peasants.

In that coming day they will all alike be children of Abraham in faith. They will be alike in their encounters with the Almighty God. They will be alike in their service for Him as sinners saved by grace, liberated and transformed to bring glory to God.

I close this chapter with the account of one more brother in Christ—a humble, joyful evangelist known widely as "Uncle Bud" Robinson.

Lost, selfish, crude, rough, profane, vulgar, alienated from God, Bud Robinson always wept when he told audiences of his great distance from God as a younger man. But then he would laugh with joy as he testified to his encounter with the God of all grace and his conversion to Christ Jesus.

"Everything looks good when Christ has come to live in your heart," Uncle Bud Robinson would say. "When the Lord filled me with the Holy Spirit, I was so blessed that I just went outside, grabbed a tree in my arms and hugged and hugged it!"

Everything looks good when you see it through the glow of worship and the aura of divine enjoyment. Bless the Lord, O my soul!

CHAPTER

3

"God Is All I Need"

Abraham's faith was from the heart and rock-solid

ULTIMATELY ABRAHAM discovered that only God matters. He discovered in that revelation the greatest concept in the world. We might say he became a "one idea" man.

I like what I see about Abraham after that.

If ever there was something significant between the lines, it is in the account of Abraham. It is as if Abraham laid hold of God's favor and promise with rejoicing, saying to himself, "When I have God, I need nothing more!"

Abraham was completely satisfied with God's friendship. He becomes to us a faithful example in his willingness to put God first. With Abraham, only God mattered.

In the fullness of time when Jesus came into the world, His emphasis to men and women was the same: "Commit your life and soul to God, for only He matters!"

To an intellectual religious leader of His day Jesus said, "If you do not know the things of the earth, how can you believe Me when I tell you about heavenly things?" (see John 3:12).

God has not changed, Christ has not changed, the need of mankind has not changed. The all-sufficient God whom Abraham discovered, whom Nicodemus sought, is just as appropriate to our aspirations today.

Abraham was not a halfhearted believer. He was completely committed to the fact that only God matters. His fellowship with God was so real that he had no problems about the spiritual/material questions raised so often in our day.

I am certain Abraham did not spend time or effort with creation theories. He discerned that the natural world is the spiritual world projected downward. The earth is the shadow of heaven. If we knew more about earth, we would know more about heaven, because the same God made them both.

It was true in Abraham's day, and it is still true that sin has scarred and polluted the earth. But God's laws from above still rule below in nature—except in the hearts of rebellious men and women.

I have long contended that the Creator God is an artist. His design and handiwork may be seen throughout His creation.

Do you have compelling memories from your childhood concerning the beauty of the earth where you grew up? I confess that I continue to think of my native Pennsylvania as a wonderful paradise of nature.

When I go back there, I still delight in the rolling green hills, the peaceful valleys, the flowing streams. I recall with pleasure the mystery in the morning fog hanging ribbon-like and low over the river, only to disappear into the sky as the sun rose.

It was not hard to sense the hand of God in the lovely face of nature all around.

And why should not we accept, not only as a matter of faith but also as a matter of common reason, that the God who made the heavens above made the earth beneath?

Abraham was a theist, and so are we if we have gone on to follow the Lord. A theist is one who believes not only that there is a God but that He is a God who loves and cares about us. He is a God who has provided a Savior as a revelation of Himself so that men and women may find Him, know Him, love Him.

In Abraham's encounter with God he learned why he was here upon earth. He was to glorify God in all things and to continually worship.

So Abraham built an altar. "The Lord appeared unto Abram, and said, Unto thy seed will I give this land: and there builded he an altar unto the Lord, who appeared unto him" (Genesis 12:7).

In our present-day age of grace and mercy, we acknowledge that the only altar in effect for us is in the glory world. It is there that our Lord Jesus Christ ministers as our great High Priest.

But we are Christian believers intent upon glorifying God and worshiping Him. It is consistent with that objective that there should be an altar deep within our own hearts, our inner beings.

Two centuries ago, George Croly captured this picture of our devotional life. We often sing his words:

Teach me to love Thee as Thine angels love,
  One holy passion filling all my frame;

The baptism of the heaven-descended Dove,
  My heart an altar, and Thy love the flame.

In many of our churches we have wooden altar
rails. Some of us have put our elbows down on
them in times of spiritual stress. But I speak here of
the need for an unseen but very real altar within our
beings. Here God will speak with us, deal with us
and teach us the joys and delights of personal communion and fellowship.

Abraham heard from God. Abraham met with
God. Abraham listened to God. Abraham responded to God. He knew the meaning of an altar
of worship and praise. Our altar of devotion and
worship within our hearts should be as real.

These truths concerning Abraham and his wholehearted response to God cause me to wonder. How
can we bring our lukewarm Christians into a realization that nothing in the world is as important to
them as God's love and God's will?

It does not take great wisdom to perceive that we
live in a generation of completely self-confident
men and women. We are doing so well and flourish-
ing in so many ways that we feel little need for God.

In spite of what God has told us about the dan-
gers of pride, we are proud, proud, proud! We are
proud of the civilization we have produced. We are
proud of our inventions, our comforts and conveniences, our educational accomplishments. We are
proud that we can travel so far and so fast.

We spend our time dashing from one place to another, pursuing business and pleasure. We assure
ourselves that the most important issue in life is

making a living. And we scarcely know what that means!

In the midst of all our hustle we try to forget that we are becoming older every day. Only an occasional man or woman has the good sense to perceive that the day of judgment draws nearer and nearer.

The Lord Jesus Christ in His earthly ministry knew all about the apathy and materialism that would dominate our lives. His words of warning were recorded by Matthew: "For what is a man profited, if he shall gain the whole world, and lose his own soul? or what shall a man give in exchange for his soul?" (16:26).

Jesus' words quoted by Luke come like an alarm to our own day and time: "Take heed to yourselves, lest at any time your hearts be overcharged with surfeiting, and drunkenness, and cares of this life, and so that day come upon you unawares. For as a snare shall it come on all them that dwell on the face of the whole earth. Watch ye therefore, and pray always, that ye may be accounted worthy to escape all these things that shall come to pass, and to stand before the Son of man" (21:34-36).

I am having a hard time trying to comprehend what has happened to sound Bible teaching. What has happened to preaching on Christian discipleship and on our daily deportment in the spiritual life? We are making an accommodation. We are offering a take-it-easy, Pollyanna type of approach that does not seem ever to have heard of total commitment to One who is our Lord and Savior.

I regret that more and more Christian believers are being drawn into a hazy, fuzzy kind of teaching that assures everyone who has ever "accepted Christ" that he or she has nothing more to be concerned about. He is OK and he will always be OK because Christ will be returning before things get too tough. Then all of us will wear our crowns, and God will see that we have cities to rule over!

If that concept is accurate, why did our Lord take the stern and unpopular position that Christian believers should be engaged in watching and praying? If there is an automatic deliverance for everyone, why did Jesus distinctly warn us to watch and pray that we might be accounted worthy to escape all the things that will come to pass?

It is my judgment that every one of us should be sure we have had that all-important encounter with God. It is an experience that leaves us delighted in our love for Him. Like Abraham, we become satisfied with the revelation that only God matters.

If you are living only to buy and sell and get gain, that is not enough. If you are living only to sleep and work, that is not enough. If you are living only to prosper and marry and raise a family, that is not enough.

If you live only to get old and die, and never find forgiveness and the daily sense of God's presence in your life, you have missed God's great purpose for you.

A great number of believers have set a limitation on what they are willing to do for the Lord, for His Church and for His people. Such an attitude only underscores the contemporary unwillingness of professing Christians to take the Word of God seriously. Their difficulty is not in understanding the

Bible but in persuading their untamed hearts to accept its plain instructions.

The question we face, therefore, is not theological. We know what the Scriptures teach. Rather, our problem is moral: Have we the courage to stand up for what we know to be true and right? Can we bring ourselves to take up the cross with its blood and death and reproach?

From Abraham's time to this very day, God has always expected that His believing people would be a separated people. Love for God and obedience to Him have always meant scorn and derision from the world.

Why should this be?

Because Abraham in his day, and the disciples of Christ in this dispensation, were friends of God. That could only mean they were pilgrims and strangers in this world and in this world's society.

Abraham was a man of faith—a godly man. He was also a lonely man. We see a revealing word picture of Abraham in Genesis 14 after he had given his nephew, Lot, the choice of the well-watered Jordan plain.

Many of the local tribes were in constant warfare. Ultimately Lot and his family were captured and taken from Sodom where they lived. One man who had escaped during the conflict went to Abraham, the Hebrew, to ask for help. This is the first time the word *Hebrew* appears in the Bible. Scholars are in agreement that the word meant "stranger" or "alien." Perhaps it was used of Abraham because he had left Ur of the Chaldees and had gone into Canaan at God's direction.

Abraham was a Hebrew, a stranger, an alien. Living in faith, living for God, he stood alone. He did not mix with the people around him. He was separated because he was God's man. He had met God. He had heard the voice of God. God had assured him of his future. He was Abraham, the Hebrew. A stranger, yes, and lonely.

Now, let me transfer this to our times and our status. The sense of not belonging is a very real part of our Christian heritage. It is easily possible that the loneliest person in the world is a Christian—given the right circumstances.

Place a believing, practicing Christian boy suddenly into the arena of an army training camp where there is no other Christian, and he is absolutely a stranger, the loneliest person in the world. The medical men and the other officers will say, "Just let him get adjusted." They always feel that the lonely person has a complex, is headed for a nervous breakdown.

But the Christian already has his values sorted out. He knows that he is a stranger. He understands why he is lonely in the midst of thousands of people around him.

We know what it means to have made our choice and to know that our Lord is our very best friend. We also know that when we break into tears from time to time, it is not a sign of weakness. It is the sense of the normal loneliness of a committed Christian in the middle of a world that rejected our Lord and now would disown us, His disciples.

Is there an encouraging word? Yes, there is a gracious word for you, fellow believer in the faith.

Being lonely in this world will only drive you to a closer communion with the God who has promised never to leave you or forsake you. He is altogether good and He is faithful. He will never break His covenant or alter that which has gone from His mouth. He has promised to keep you as the apple of His eye. He has promised to watch over you as a mother watches over her child.

God's anxiety for you is real, and His pattern for you is plain. He says, "This is the sign of your pleasing My indwelling Spirit: you have been absorbed with Christ, you have made your thoughts a clean sanctuary for His holy habitation."

Build that invisible altar within. Let the Spirit of God produce the living, cleansing flame that marks your devotion to Christ, our Lord.

4

"Let the Fresh Waters Flow"

Isaac reopened the old wells—an object lesson for us

WHAT GOOD IS A WELL that is stopped up or dry? Isaac, second in the line of Hebrew patriarchs, must have asked that question many times. If you doubt it, look at the record in Genesis 26.

The answer, I am sure, was always the same. A stopped up, dry well is of no value to anyone until it is re-dug and cleaned out so the fresh water is again available.

At least at one point in his life, Isaac showed great concern for the unused, stopped-up wells that his father Abraham earlier had dug.

Reflecting on Isaac and his well-digging afford us opportunity to consider some of the fountainheads in our Christian assemblies that are stopped up and dry. Once they were channels intended to be blessings. But the water has ceased to flow.

As we follow our emphasis on genuine Christian experience, we can profit by considering what keeps us from meeting God in daily Bible meditation and private prayer. From my observation, I fear there is very little fresh water flowing from the wells of scriptural confession and reconciliation.

In our churches, we Christians shy away from such unpopular subjects as self-discipline and serious, wholehearted commitment. Surely those wells need to be reopened if we are to be pleasing to our Lord.

Have you heard anything lately concerning scriptural contrition of heart and the great need for true repentance? The devil, that old and ancient enemy of our souls, makes it his important business to stop up the wells of spiritual blessing and Christian experience. He is trying his best to sell Christians short, suggesting that these channels of blessing are now ancient and out-of-date. He would have us believe they should be allowed to dry up to a trickle and finally be abandoned altogether.

We will consider these issues within the framework of Isaac's experiences, so first let's look briefly at the record of his life and his testimony for God.

It is only fair to admit that we do not remember Isaac in the same way we do his father Abraham. But we should not be surprised that the mature Isaac became God's man in his generation. Although he never attained the stature of his father, he had his personal encounters with the Lord.

What young man had a more memorable, dramatic exierence of God's dealings with people than the boy Isaac? Taken by his father at God's bidding to a distant mountaintop where the Lord had said he should be sacrificed, Isaac asked, "Father, you have everything ready for the sacrifice, but where is the lamb—the animal to be slain?"

And Abraham answered, "The Lord will provide!"

But it was Isaac, not a lamb, who was tied to that altar of sacrifice. An angel intervened, halting God's test of Abraham's faith. And, sure enough, a ram from a nearby thicket became the sacrifice.

As Isaac grew older, what do you suppose he would have replied to anyone who suggested that his father's God was not real, not alive?

"Do not tell me that God is not a living God," I suspect he would have replied. "Do not tell me my father's God is not real. I remember well the day I was on the altar. I know very well the faith of my father Abraham. I live today because God lives and cares. I am aware that I am known personally to Him!"

The Genesis record tells us that during a time of famine, Isaac started moving toward Egypt with his flocks, as Abraham had done years earlier. Ultimately he reached the land of Gerar. There the Lord appeared to him and told him not to go to Egypt, but to stay in Gerar, where Abimilech ruled.

After making an agreement with the king, Isaac pitched his tents in the valley of Gerar. Immediately he started locating and re-digging the wells that his father had dug years before. These were wells that the enemy Philistines, after the death of Abraham, had filled in and made useless. Now, as Isaac and his servants began opening them, producing potable water, they were challenged by the local herdsmen.

"This water is ours," the herdsmen contended.

Isaac was not a fighting man. He just wanted room for his family and his flocks. So he picked up his tents and moved on to the site of another well. When Isaac finally dug a flowing well and there was neither challenge nor conflict, he called it Rehobeth, meaning that God had made room for him.

"Now the Lord has made room for us," he said to his household. "We shall be fruitful in the land."

Later, going up to Beersheba, Isaac was visited by the Lord, who said, "Fear not, for I am with thee, and will bless thee" (Genesis 26:24). Isaac immediately did two things, and I believe that each had its own significance.

First, he built an altar and worshiped, calling on the name of the Lord. Then, with his servants, he dug another well!

Isaac remembered his boyhood and the wells of flowing water. That part of the world has always been arid. Isaac knew very well that fresh, flowing water was not just an option. It was a necessity. And here is where we tie in these actions of Isaac with the Christian life.

We are on familiar ground in the fourth chapter of John's Gospel, where Jesus spoke to the Samaritan woman at Jacob's well. "Whosoever drinketh of this water shall thirst again," He said: "But whosoever drinketh of the water that I shall give him shall never thirst; but the water that I shall give him shall be in him a well of water springing up into everlasting life" (4:13-14).

In his day, the Old Testament prophet Isaiah had used a like figure. "Ho, every one that thirsteth, come ye to the waters, and he that hath no money; come" (55:1).

The underground streams of water in our world are a free gift of God. Mankind could never create the natural flow of water. It is there by the provision of Almighty God, the Creator. Man must dig his wells to tap the water source, to get down where the water flows. Once released, the water blesses God's creation.

Think of the wells of water representing the doctrines, methods and channels we use to obtain the water of life—salvation through Jesus Christ—God's free gift to a sinning, dying world. For us, the flow began when our Lord Jesus Christ opened His great heart as He died on Calvary's cross.

With God's help, I want to make the application of Bible truth practical and helpful. The first practical question is: Who will reopen these wells?

You may be tempted to suggest that we pray and ask God to open the wells. No! No!

God had put the water in the ground at Gerar and Beersheba, and there was plenty more where it came from. But God did not tell Isaac to go lie down under a cactus and rest while He did the digging.

For our Christian blessings, God has already made full provision in the atoning death of Jesus Christ and in the supernatural ministries of the Holy Spirit. God has given us spiritual tools—the abilities to trust Him and to believe Him and to obey Him. He has also given us intelligence to realize what we ought to do and how we can lay hold of His blessings.

People are slow to take God at His Word. I would not be faithful to my commission if I did not remind you that men and women are now in hell who had the belief that God was going to do for them what only they could do for themselves. They have gone out into eternity without ever having said, "Jesus, I come." They wanted God to do what He specifically had told them to do!

God saw fit to create us as individuals, and it is as individuals that we are responsible and accountable to God. If we are believing Christians, God has given us many responsibilities that relate to our own spiritual blessing and maturity. He has also given us responsibilities that relate to the spiritual good of the community of Christians where we have been placed.

Friend, we must dig out the old wells! We must recognize our dryness of spirit, our coldness of heart. We must make the decision to renew our desire for God, for the outpouring of His Spirit and for the seasons of rejoicing as we become more like Jesus.

Many a congregation has been renewed and blessed when believers have been willing to reopen the Bible wells of reconciliation and confession. When Christians are harboring hard feelings against each other, they need to be reconciled. They need to confess and ask forgiveness.

I refer here to actual sins and faults. There are people in continual bondage to mere trifles and inconsequential matters. God has given us the Holy Spirit to be our prompter and our guide. And He has given us good sense as well to go along with our consciences.

In sincere and honest confession, two areas are involved. If you have sinned and wronged someone, you need to take the matter to the Lord first and receive His forgiveness. Then you need to go to the person you have wronged and ask his or her forgiveness.

I am not in agreement with the practice of making confessions public knowledge. Why should we encourage people to stand in front of the entire congregation to confess their embarrassing life histories?

I have followed this as a sound formula over the years: Tell God in earnest prayer, then go to the person you have wronged. These private matters do not need to be shouted from the housetops. Even your pastor does not need the details. Let your confession be made honestly to God, and then follow through with the one you have wronged.

Something more needs to be said about reconciliation among Christians. The Bible admonishes us to live in peace with everyone, but with two gracious little disclaimers: "If it be possible" and "as much as lieth in you" (Romans 12:18).

If you have ever thought you could succeed in getting everyone to love you, think again! There are some people with whom you cannot live in peace and keep your conscience right. Do the best you can, and do not worry about them. The old saints said, "Tell the truth and shame the devil." If in shaming the devil with the truth you wound someone who refuses to forgive, live in peace as much as lies in your power. Remember that Jesus died with some people hating Him.

Now, let me observe that some Christians think they can be disciples of Christ without ever a thought about the necessity of self-discipline and genuine commitment to Him. We must face the fact that many today are notoriously careless in their living. This attitude finds its way into the church. We have liberty, we have money, we live in comparative luxury. As a result, discipline practically has disappeared.

What would a violin solo sound like if the strings on the musician's instrument were all hanging loose, not stretched tight, not "disciplined"? Being an artist, the musician would not attempt to bring sound from that violin until each string had been tuned and tested and all was in perfect harmony.

In things that matter with God—important things—we need to be disciplined, pulled together, attuned to the Spirit until we are in harmony with all of God's planning for us.

Are you asking what kind of medieval doctrine this is? How could we be more up-to-date than to be praying that we accept God's disciplines for our lives? God expects us to wisely use our time. He wants us to repent for our carelessness and laziness in matters of the Spirit.

You can reject this concept of wholehearted commitment to Jesus Christ if you wish. But this is a very good well to be unstopped. Our fathers found refreshing water in it!

I want to emphasize another important well—one of the most neglected. It has to do with spiritual progress and victory. Our fathers found that God's instructions could be trusted. "Cease to do evil. Learn to do good." God has never changed His instructions about repentance. When we come to God, contrite and in believing faith, there is bound to be a moral housecleaning. And we are not even coming close to talking about legalism!

In His ministry, Jesus taught plainly that repentance is not just for the bad, bad few. He said about the Galileans on whom the tower fell, "Suppose ye

that these Galilaeans were sinners above all the Galilaeans, because they suffered such things? I tell
you, Nay: but, except ye repent, ye shall all likewise
perish" (Luke 13:2-3).

There are many peculiar ideas about biblical repentance. I have talked with people who tried to tell
me that repentance is necessary because "it makes
you fit so that God can save you." The Bible does
not teach that, and it never did. No man or woman
has changed the character and goodness of God by
an act of repentance. All the repentance in the universe cannot make God any more loving, any more
gracious. Repentance is not a meritorious act. God
is eternally good, and He welcomes us into His
love, grace and mercy when we meet His condition
of an about-face so that we are aware of His smile.

Repentance means turning around from our evil
ways in order to look to Jesus. The person who will
not repent still has his or her back turned on God.

Repentance is a condition we meet in order that
God, already wanting to be good to us, can be good
to us, forgiving and cleansing us. In that sense,
then, the man who loves his sin and hangs on to it
cannot reasonably expect the goodness and the
grace of God.

We who are forgiven and justified sinners sensed
in our own repentance only a token of the wounding and the chastisement that fell on our Lord Jesus
Christ as He stood in our place. A truly penitent
person does not feel he or she dares to ask God to
let him or her off. But peace has been established.
The blows fell on Jesus. This gracious message from
God that there is a substitionary atonement through
the finished work of our Lord Jesus Christ is the

good news that "with his stripes we are healed" (Isaiah 53:5).

Another thing. There are many, many today who are passing by the need for spiritual training. They see not the necessity of forming right religious habits. They do not realize that we must wrestle against the world, the flesh and the devil. They have become so assured that they are saints by call that they seek not to be saints by character.

If we think of repentance as something we do only once in our Christian experience, we need to get the well open again. We need to dig out the rubbish and get the water flowing once more.

Probably the most important discipline we have abandoned is meditation in God's Word, related as it is to the necessity for private prayer. How well I know from my own experience that Satan is always busy stopping up the well of private prayer. Not one of us among God's children is immune to this danger of losing out in our prayer life.

I knew of an able preacher greatly used of the Lord in evangelism and Bible conferences. He was a busy, busy man. There came the occasion when someone frankly asked him, "Doctor, tell us about your prayer life. How do you pray? How much do you pray?"

The man was embarrassed as he replied, "I must confess to you something I have not confessed before. I do not have the time to pray as I used to. My time alone with God has been neglected."

Not too long afterward, that preacher sustained a serious failure. It brought his ministry to an abrupt end, and he was put on the shelf.

If we want to be honest with God, we will take

solemnly the admonition to pray without ceasing. God's work on this earth languishes when God's people give up their ministries of prayer and supplication. I cannot tell you why this is true, but it *is* true.

What about the power of God's Word in your life? Have you been spiritually blessed through meditating on it? Do you find Bible study a delight? Perhaps that well is also stopped up!

If we will thoughtfully read the Bible, we will find it the source of great grace. I remember James M. Gray, the noted Bible teacher, telling of a Christian brother, a Michigan farmer, whose spiritual life had suddenly blossomed until there was an overflowing of God's presence. Many in the man's community recognized the change in his life and personality and sought spiritual counsel from him. Dr. Gray had opportunity to ask the man about the transformation of his spiritual life and witness.

"Dr. Gray, I began to devote myself to the Scriptures for my own need," the man humbly explained. "Something happened when God opened my spiritual understanding as I studied the book of Ephesians. I cannot really explain what the Lord is doing for me and through me, but it has come through prayerful meditation in the Word of God."

None of us can expect to get the rich, transforming blessings from God apart from the Scriptures. The Scriptures are a deep, flowing well in themselves.

Too many of us ministers and Sunday school teachers are content to reach for a commentary on the Scriptures. What we need most is to search the Scriptures for ourselves. If we have a tender, obedient, prayerful heart, the Holy Spirit will tell us about the text. He is the kind of help we need!

I hope you are not bragging that you have no doubts or fears. God does not want us to be hypocrites. He expects us to be realists.

I heard about an old Christian man who testified, "I'll admit that I sometimes have doubts. But I always take them to God immediately. I just dive down to the bottom and examine the foundations of my faith. That tactic has not failed yet. Always I have come to the surface singing "How firm a foundation, ye saints of the Lord, / Is laid for your faith in His excellent Word."

That quite well sums up all that I have been trying to say. The believer who takes his or her spiritual problems to God and to His Word will always be the spiritually refreshed believer!

"God Is Really Here"

Jacob finds the face of God turned manward

THE MAN JACOB, WHOM we study in the pages of Genesis with much interest, has been described by a religious writer as "one of the Bible's most colorful characters." With that description we agree.

But I do not propose this to be just a biographical study of this colorful character. Rather, I want to center on the one thing in Jacob's life important to us now.

Simply stated, here it is: Jacob had personal, transforming encounters with the God of his fathers.

In the early stages of his life, Jacob seemed hopeless. We cannot read very far before coming to the conclusion that Jacob was a cheat and a crook. He operated carnally and selfishly. He seemingly had no desire to find God's will for his life. We first come to regard Jacob as anything but a worthy character.

In this era of grace, we dwell heavily on the New Testament teachings of God's love, mercy and faithfulness. It is fitting, therefore, that we turn to the

Old Testament record of God's dealings with Jacob. Nowhere will the man or woman who has fallen short of the glory of God find greater encouragement.

I do not intend to psychoanalyze Jacob. But I must say that as a young man he already had three strikes against him. And that is when a person is generally removed from the game.

First, Jacob's home life was unfortunate. While Isaac and Rebekah never separated or divorced, throughout their marriage they were woefully divided. Their hearts were not knit together in loving unity.

Rebekah had a habit of eavesdropping when Isaac, her husband, would be talking with either Jacob or Esau. Then she would hurry to the other son with her own words and schemes. And so trouble developed. To be reared in a home situation like that was strike one against Jacob.

We notice also the favoritism shown by the parents. Isaac loved Esau because he was a hunter and brought home savory venison. That is a poor reason for loving anyone. But Isaac loved Esau because of the venison.

On the other hand, Rebekah loved Jacob because he "was a plain man, dwelling in tents" (Genesis 25:27). I take that to mean he was content to stay around home with his mother. Perhaps she valued him for the great stews he learned to cook.

That was strike two—being tied to his mother's apron strings.

Looking beyond the household to Jacob's own person, we observe that he matured with many

moral flaws. There were weaknesses in his character beyond the normal.

There was duplicity, there was dishonesty, there
was greed. He cheated his own brother. He cheated
his father. And he went on to cheat his father-in-
law. Jacob seemed to be completely lacking in what
we would call common honor. He showed a spirit of
disloyalty and faithlessness in dealing with his
brother and his father.

That was strike three. As far as morality and
honor and honesty are concerned, Jacob was out of
the game.

I think we can safely say that the Jacob of those
earlier years would have been voted the man least
likely to get right with God. If we had been his
judge and jury, we would have pronounced him
hopeless.

But of all those looking at Jacob, there was One
who disagreed. That One was God. God, with His
eternal omniscience, saw in Jacob something worth-
while.

As a human being, I am amazed at this point.
There is deep mystery here—mystery that none of
us can understand. God kept after Jacob, continuing to trouble him, to pursue him.

Some years ago I wrote a book that is still being
sold. My thesis in that book is that we must seek
God and follow hard after Him. I told the publisher
the title should be *The Pursuit of God*. Someone tried
to get me to change the title. "People will not read a
book about the pursuit of God," he argued. But
those were the very words that caught the imagina-
tion of the reading public.

The story of Jacob and the stories of other similar

characters in the Bible have caused me to believe I could write a sequel entitled *God's Pursuit of Man*. Before any person can begin seriously to pursue God, God must first pursue him or her. Before anyone can begin seriously to seek God, God must already have begun to seek him or her.

Always God must be previous. God must be there first!

God knew Jacob better than anyone else knew him. And God did not consider Jacob a hopeless case. God appeared to Jacob in personal encounter, even though Jacob was not seeking God up to that time.

Jacob's condition of soul and mind as he began his eventful journey from Canaan to Haran must have been that of a man under deep conviction of soul, hopeless in his alienation. The world that he thought was his to control by guile and deception suddenly had fallen apart. He had just deceived and cheated his aged, blind father. Setting out from home for a distant land, he could only have wondered if he would ever see Isaac again.

Then, too, his strong, hairy brother Esau, whom he had cheated out of his birthright and then out of his father's blessing, was making serious threats to kill him. Mother Rebekah, the instigator of Jacob's most serious deception, had advised Jacob's departure, arguing her desire that he take a wife in the country from which she came.

Jacob well knew he was not going after a wife. He was going away in haste to save his own crooked hide.

Probably it would be difficult to find anywhere in

history a more miserable or more lonely man than
Jacob as he left mother and father and home.

Knowing the lives of Abraham and Isaac, we can
surely believe there had been religious teaching in
Isaac's household. Jacob must have known about
the covenant-making God of his grandfather Abraham and the God of his father Isaac. We must conclude that Jacob, as he began his journey to Haran,
not only hated himself for what he was and for
what he had done, but he felt an inner longing for
the knowledge and presence of God. Only God
could answer his human need.

I think Jacob had come to a place of inner crisis in
which he was self-stricken, hating himself for his
sins and his flaws. He at last discovered that he had
joined the great army of the discontented. Those
conditions and that attitude added up to a deep, un-
satisfied longing after God.

The person who is spiritually discontented has
good reason to thank God with all his or her heart.
Most people in our world have a feeling they are
"good enough." They are complacent. They are
quite well satisfied with themselves. Not bad
enough to be much troubled by their consciences,
they have no longing after God.

Jacob probably had never been away from home
before. Traveling north from Beersheba with his
lonely and miserable thoughts, he stopped at the
end of the day and prepared for nightfall. I have
never been able to figure out why he took stones for
his pillows. Maybe he wanted to lean back against
them as he thought on and on about his troubles
until he fell asleep.

During the night, God dealt with Jacob in a

dream, giving him a vivid vision of a ladder stretch-
ing from earth to heaven. Angels ascended and descended the ladder, apparently interested in Jacob's
welfare. Then the voice of the Lord came to him
with a positive message:

> "I am the Lord God of Abraham thy father, and
> the God of Isaac: the land whereon thou liest, to
> thee will I give it, and to thy seed; and thy seed
> shall be as the dust of the earth, and thou shalt
> spread abroad to the west, and to the south: and
> in thee and in thy seed shall all the families of the
> earth be blessed. And, behold, I am with thee,
> and will keep thee in all places whither thou
> goest, and will bring thee again into this land; for
> I will not leave thee, until I have done that which I
> have spoken to thee of" (Genesis 28:13-15).

When Jacob awakened from his sleep, he said,
"Surely the Lord is in this place; and I knew it not."

Jacob did more than to awake from physical slum-
ber. The heavenly vision and the voice of the Lord
became a sudden awakening of the inner life. It
used to be said of a person who was converted to
Christ that he or she had had a spiritual awakening.
There is no better way to put it.

Jacob had lived with the thought that he con-
trolled his world. Suddenly he found himself con-
fronted by the God who made the world and who
sustains it by the word of His power. God is in His
world, and many people still do not know it.

In awaking, Jacob did not say, "God came here."
With a new awareness and conviction he said,
"God is here. This is the gate of heaven." God had

been there all the time. The problem was that Jacob did not know it.

So Jacob awoke to the presence of God. There at lonely Bethel he discovered the shining knowledge of a personal God. He became aware that God was and is in the world He created.

But where do you and I find God?

I rejoice to tell you that Christ is our meeting place. The angels long ago announced it when they said that His name should be Immanuel—God with us. Our Lord Jesus Christ is the manward side of God. I repeat it, for you may not hear anyone else saying it: our Lord Jesus Christ is the manward side of God.

Let me illustrate this in a practical, understandable way. Often you and I have looked into the night sky and seen a bright moon. We personify the object of our gaze by imagining we see a so-called man-in-the-moon. That moon is so situated in relation to the earth that we always see its same side. It is impossible for us to look upward from the earth and see its other side.

Throughout all of mankind's history on this planet, we have seen the same side of the moon. Adam saw it in his day. Abraham saw it when he left Ur of the Chaldees. Jacob saw it as he journeyed to Haran. Perhaps they, too, imagined the face of a man-in-the-moon! It is the moon's earthward side.

Just as our moon has an earthward side, I assure you that God in His great heaven has a side that is manward. It is the side that is turned to us. It is the only side we see. The God who pursued Jacob in the wastes of the wilderness, the God who has been so faithful in following up us, has a manward side, and His name is Jesus!

When we look up in faith, we see the everlasting face of God revealed in Jesus Christ!

The saints of God throughout the ages have known about the manward side of God. They knew that manward side was Jesus Christ. Jesus plainly told the Jews of New Testament time, "Your father Abraham rejoiced to see my day: and he saw it, and was glad" (John 8:56). Moses prophesied concerning Jesus, and Isaiah saw Him exalted and enthroned. Simeon, encountering the infant Jesus at the temple, recognized Him as God's Messiah.

Surely John the Baptist would like to get his word of confirmation in here. Who could have any stronger utterance than John about God's plan for showing His manward side in Jesus Christ? John was God's chosen instrument to prepare the way for the Savior.

John was a true prophet of God. He had a ministry to perform, and the sharp sword of the Lord was in his mouth. He cried, "Repent ye: for the kingdom of heaven is at hand" (Matthew 3:2).

Great throngs followed this rough-clothed man from the wilderness, and the hearts of many were turned God-ward and prepared spiritually for Messiah's coming.

John's last public words were probably the most beautiful and the most prophetic of all those that had marked his ministry. After Jesus' earthly work had begun, some of John's followers began to compare John's record of baptisms with the number of baptisms Jesus was performing. They came to John with questions.

"What is happening, John?" they asked. "Are you being crowded out? Is this Newcomer trying to take your place?"

I must admit that I am blessed every time I reread those final words of John the Baptist. "I am not the Christ, but . . . I am sent before him. He that hath the bride is the bridegroom: but the friend of the bridegroom, which standeth and heareth him, rejoiceth greatly because of the bridegroom's voice: this my joy therefore is fulfilled. He must increase, but I must decrease" (John 3:28-30). John condensed into that one final sentence the secret of his own spiritual greatness: "Jesus must increase, but I must decrease."

Abraham. Isaac. Jacob. Moses. Isaiah. John the Baptist. All of these knew that God had a face turned manward. They knew that God is here. They knew it through experience.

Oh, what a delight to know that Jesus Christ is the point at which we experience God! For it was Jesus Himself who told His generation, "He that hath seen me hath seen the Father" (John 14:9). The message remains unchanged.

"I Will Not Let Thee Go"

Wounded Jacob is renewed by his hunger for God

IT IS AMAZING to me! There are people within the ranks of Christianity who have been taught and who believe that Christ will shield His followers from wounds of every kind.

If the truth were known, the saints of God in every age were only effective after they had been wounded. They experienced the humbling wounds that brought contrition, compassion and a yearning for the knowledge of God. I could only wish that more among the followers of Christ knew what some of the early saints meant when they spoke of being wounded by the Holy Spirit.

Think for a moment about the apostle Paul. I suppose there is no theologian living or dead who quite knows what Paul meant when he said, "From henceforth let no man trouble me: for I bear in my body the marks of the Lord Jesus" (Galatians 6:17). Every commentary has a different idea. I think Paul referred to the wounds he suffered because of his faith and godly life.

When we return to Old Testament Jacob, whose experiences we were considering in the previous chapter, we see a young man who for years had operated in his own sphere of life without wounds. He was a true Jew. He knew that he was intelligent. He knew that as long as he could get around unwounded, he would come through every skirmish on top of the heap. It was not a question of his being proud or vain. He just knew that in matters of this world he was good.

Jacob prospered in Haran. He gained not only a wife but wives. And children. And flocks and herds. After 20 years, he decided he would return with his family and his possessions to his own country.

Jacob was still worried, however, about meeting Esau, his brother. Learning enroute that Esau was coming to meet him with a sizeable contingent of 400 men did not ease Jacob's fears.

Sending his family before sunset across the ford of the river Jabbok, Jacob remained behind alone. There at the ford of the Jabbok, Jacob encountered a heavenly Being. The Scriptures simply say, "There wrestled a man with him until the breaking of the day" (Genesis 32:24). In the darkness of that Middle Eastern night, Jacob wrestled.

At daybreak, the Stranger touched Jacob's thigh, wounding him, putting the thigh out of joint. But still Jacob wrestled.

"I will not let thee go, except thou bless me," Jacob vowed.

"What is thy name?" the Man asked.

"Jacob." The name means schemer, supplanter, literally, heel grabber. It fit Jacob's character exactly.

The Visitor replied, "Thy name shall be called no more Jacob, but Israel: for as a prince hast thou power with God and with men, and hast prevailed." And He gave Jacob the blessing Jacob had wrestled for. Jacob called the name of the ford Peniel. He said, "I have seen God face to face, and my life is preserved."

At Peniel Jacob was wounded. The Bible informs us that for the rest of his life "he halted upon his thigh"—he limped. But the Bible informs us of something else. It says that as Jacob passed across the ford of the Jabbok, "the sun rose upon him." Before, Jacob had been in the shadows so much of the time that the sun had difficulty reaching his troubled face!

And about his wound. Certainly we would agree that the matter of a limp for the rest of his life was a very small price to pay for the benefits of a wound administered by the Lord Himself.

From the hurried glimpses we have seen of Jacob in this chapter and the last, I want to consider some spiritual lessons to be drawn from the lives and attitudes of Jacob and his twin brother Esau.

If we had been neighbors to the household of Isaac and Rebekah and dependent only on our human judgment, we very probably would have selected Esau above Jacob as the brother more likely to succeed. We would have agreed that Esau was a good and promising young man.

To be sure, he had some rough edges, we would have said, but overall he had what it takes. He was a hunter and he was active and red-blooded. He smelled of the fields and the outdoors. He was kind to his parents. His character was unquestioned. His reputation was good.

On the other hand, everyone seemed to know about Jacob's moral shortcomings. If we were living in the same tent with Jacob, we would lock up our valuables at night. With scheming, cheating Jacob around, a person could not be too careful.

No, if we had to pick Jacob or Esau to live with, we would have picked Esau at that time in their lives.

But it turned out that Jacob had something Esau never possessed. Jacob had an inner longing for God. Yes, Jacob was deep in sin, but when it came to the time of soul crisis, he felt the tug and the lift of another, better world.

By comparison, Esau's controlling vice was his continuing and complete self-satisfaction. The thing that damned him was his spiritual complacency, his satisfaction and contentment in being just what he was. He had no desire to change, to be godly, to be God's man.

Knowing his own many faults and flaws, Jacob sensed within himself a great dissatisfaction. In every generation, the people who have found God have been those who have come to the end of themselves. Recognizing their hopelessness, they have been ready to throw themselves on the mercy and grace of a forgiving God.

Numbers of people come to me not to discuss their talents and abilities, but to talk about their flaws and their spiritual yearnings for God. That encourages me, and it should encourage any pastor. We ministers can do little to help a person whose discontent is with things: job, circumstances, possessions or their lack. That which we cherish is the discontent with the condition of the soul and inner spirit. We welcome the one who has a deep-seated longing for God and a yearning to live more pleasing to Him.

God had been faithful in trying to get His signals through to Jacob and Esau. Esau was so intent upon the things of earth and flesh that he heeded them not. He was satisfied, content. Let everything continue as it is, was his attitude; that's fine! Never mind the voice of God trying to get through.

I sense a description of the humanness of Esau in the words of the poet Browning about a man he called "a finished and finite clod, not troubled by a spark." That is a terribly condemning epitaph: "A finished and finite clod"!

How many people in our world today are all done—finished, never to change? No one is going to work on them anymore. They are clods. Finite. Finished. Never any spark within and never any response to what God is trying to do.

It is the spark of God within a person that troubles him or her. That spark is placed within by the Spirit of God. Conviction. Longing. Desire.

That spark within does not save. But that spark must be there to lead the person on to salvation.

Why is it that some men and women seem never to have any awareness of that spark from God? They may be nice people, nice neighbors, nice friends. But they live every day without any spark of discontent, without any spark of need for God.

I sense that Esau was that kind of finished clod. And I note with grief the caution voiced in the letter to the Hebrews:

Looking diligently lest any man fail of the grace of God; lest any root of bitterness springing up trouble you, and thereby many be defiled; lest there be any fornicator, or profane person, as Esau, who for one morsel of meat sold his birthright. For ye know how that afterward, when he would have inherited the blessing, he was rejected: for he found no place of repentance, though he sought it carefully with tears (12:15-17).

In the Genesis account of Jacob and Esau, we are in touch with the faithful overshadowing of God, the eternal Mystery, in the life of Jacob. We do not sense that the same can be said of Esau. He was not bothered. He was not longing for that Presence which goes beyond the physical satisfactions of food and drink and family and friends.

Do not ever forget that God has made us with the right to make our own choices. We were not created to be robots. God made us in His own image, but with the right and the ability to choose. We are free moral agents.

When our first parents made the wrong choices, the human race became alienated from God. Since that time, every person has been faced with choices and decisions. The person who wants to be God's man or woman has to *choose* to follow the Lord. God's invitations are found throughout the Bible. He has never ceased saying, "Come unto Me."

Each person has to make the decision to take God at His word. When that happens, his or her heart closes down tight upon the Word of God. The person testifies, "I have chosen the way of truth!"

This is one point where we have to be dogmatic.

There is only one way to God, and the choice must be made. There is no other way to get into the kingdom of God. If a person does not make the choice to enter, he or she will never get in.

Jacob made his choice and became one of God's men. Esau did not choose. He never did decide.

Esau represents a large company of people in the world today. They keep on assuring themselves that they will "make it" into the kingdom of God by a kind of heavenly osmosis. They have a fond hope that there is a kind of unconscious "leaking through" of their personalities into the walls of the kingdom.

That is a vain hope. No one ever comes to God by an automatic or unconscious process. It does not happen like that at all. The individual man or woman must make the choice. On that we must be dogmatic!

We have the Book, the Word of God. We know that God has revealed Himself as our God. We know that God has offered Himself through His giving of Jesus Christ, the eternal Son. We know that the saving message is the gospel—the good news—of our Lord Jesus Christ. We know that we have had an authentic experience of the grace and mercy of God. We have made our decision. Our own hearts, like bear traps, have clamped down on God's gracious offer. In our rejoicing we have said, "This is it! We have chosen! This is it!"

There is no way that God can come to us and help us until we make the choice. There is no way that He can forgive us, cleanse us and restore us to the position of son or daughter until we consciously let Him.

The Lord has been waiting long and patiently for a great company of people who say they are searching. They are having their own way. They claim to be "testing." The tragedy is that most of them are related to Esau. They are satisfied with things as they find them. They will never come to a point of decision. They will never choose to be God's men, God's women.

The worst part is the fact that so many of them are holding back because "we don't want to give up our freedom." That is one of the great fallacies held by unbelievers—thinking that the Christian must surrender his or her freedom in order to be a Christian. The notion is one of Satan's inventions, but it is still effective in our day. The devil is able to make sinners imagine they are free!

But it is the Christian who is really free. The Christian has liberty from his or her burden of guilt. The Christian is free from the nasty temper and human jealousies. The Christian is free from slavery to alcohol, tobacco and other substances. Best of all, the Christian is finally free from a thousand fears, including the fear of death and hell.

The unsaved person is hanging on to his or her freedom to sin, to pile up judgment, to get old and to die without God.

What about you? Can it be that you are satisfied spiritually because you are not uneasy about anything? You can hear a strong Bible sermon or an appealing gospel song, and they do not even scratch the surface of your emotions. You manage to let the television entertain you until midnight, you sleep, you eat a hearty breakfast and go to work—entirely untroubled by any spark. You are satisfied with yourself and with the things that compose your earthly life.

There are two great evils apparent among us today. The two are related in that both spring from callous, apathetic human attitudes. The first is the prevailing spirit of impenitence. The second is the total willingness to exist day after day without any longing for God.

If we yearned after God even as much as a cow yearns for her calf, we would be the worshiping and effective believers God wants us to be. If we longed for God as a bride looks forward to the return of her husband, we would be a far greater force for God than we are now.

Our hindrance, our difficulty is our lack of desire for God. We have reduced this entire spiritual matter to a kind of mail-order, automatic acquisition: Christ died on the cross. I believe He died for me. Now I have nothing to do but wait for His return and He will give me a big, bright crown.

Let me tell you, there will be some bitter disappointments in that coming day when we find how wrong we have been. We have tried to reduce our relationship to God to an automatic coin-in-the-slot proposition. And it will not work that way.

I remind you that we live in a spiritually troubled time in history. Christianity has gone over to the jingle-bell crowd. Everyone is just delighted that Jesus has done all of the sorrowing, all of the suffering, all of the dying.

Christian believers are emphasizing happiness. They no longer want to hear what the Bible says about death to self and the life of spiritual victory through identification with Christ in His death and resurrection. The number is great of those who will no longer admit that spiritual victory often comes through wrestling in a long, dark night of the soul.

"That is not for us," they contend. "Jesus did all of the suffering so we can be happy. And we are going to be happy even if we have to invent new ways to happiness!"

The worst part is that we also expect Jesus will do all of the loving. We have largely forgotten the first and great commandment, "Thou shalt love the Lord thy God with all thy heart, and with all thy soul, and with all thy mind."

What I am anxious to see in Christian believers is a beautiful paradox. I want to see in them the joy of finding God while at the same time they are blessedly pursuing Him. I want to see in them the great joy of having God and yet always wanting Him!

"Why This Burning Bush?"

To be God's man, Moses had to experience God personally

THE WORD PORTRAIT of Moses in the Old Testament is summed up well in Exodus 33:11. There the Bible says, "The Lord spake unto Moses face to face, as a man speaketh unto his friend."

One of the important conversations between the Lord and Moses is preserved for us in Exodus 3, when Moses turned aside in wonder to see why a burning bush was not consumed by the fire within it. Out of the bush came the voice of the Lord telling Moses that he had been chosen for the difficult task of liberating the Hebrew nation from slavery in Egypt.

Moses was an effective emancipator, liberating an entire nation from the grinding slavery of the Egyptian Pharaohs. Moses was a prophet. It was said of Christ that He was a prophet like unto Moses. Moses had a major role in the establishment of God's Law, the greatest moral code ever given to mankind.

It is difficult to overstate the greatness of the man or the brilliance of his career.

We should quickly review here the kinds of preparation Moses had gone through for his leadership role under God. Reared in Pharaoh's palace, he had been educated in all the wisdom of the Egyptians. He had the prerequisites for almost any kind of career. In our day a man with his qualifications would be sought for election as a bishop or the president of any of the great church denominations.

Then, too, Moses had a most unusual but highly effective postgraduate course. God took him out of the activity and the noise of Egypt and placed him in the silence of the open spaces. He kept the flock of Jethro, his father-in-law. Tending the sheep, he learned lessons of meditation and observation that he could only have learned in the silence.

Probably more important than anything else, Moses learned to know himself. That knowledge was a part of God's preparation of the man for his future tasks. We, today, know everything but ourselves. We never really come to know ourselves because we cannot get quiet enough.

I have thought much about Moses spending those evening hours alone with his sheep. There is an old proverb that says, "If you would be alone, look at the stars."

It was Emerson who commented that if the stars should come out only one night in a thousand years, everyone would drop what he or she was doing and in awe "look at the shining city of God." But because we see them all the time and because we are busy, we pay very little attention to the stars. We have too much noise and too many distractions!

Yes, Moses was a man unusually qualified to embark on one of the great undertakings of history. But in God's eyes his preparation was still not complete. God was planning an incident, an event, in which Moses would come into personal encounter with Himself, the living, eternal God.

It was God's plan that Moses should learn an overpowering sense of reverence in a dramatic person-to-Person encounter with Deity. Moses' preparation could not be complete without such a meeting.

Coming to this Exodus text that relates the experience of Moses at the burning bush, we discern that God first revealed Himself to Moses as fire. God is inscrutable and ineffable. There is no way He can really tell us who and what He is. He can only tell us what He is like. In this instance we learn that He is like fire.

Some groups in the world have believed that God *is* fire. So they have worshiped the flame of fire burning on their altars.

We have many human ways to ignite a fire. And fire is indiscriminatory. Fire can burn a building or cook a stew. God is not fire, but He is like fire. Fire is the nearest comparison God can use to illustrate to His poor, half-blind children what He is like.

To Moses, God appeared as fire. Moses knelt down in awe and reverence as God spoke to him out of the bush.

I think we are agreed that Moses had an overwhelming experience in that personal encounter with God. He received God's commission to deliver Israel. And ultimately he would receive the Law of God and organize the great Hebrew nation from which Messiah would come. All of this because Moses met God.

Previously, God had been just a good and pleasant idea to Moses. The idea of God is a distant and nebulous concept, and the average person tries to deal with it on the basis of intellect. As an orthodox Hebrew, Moses' idea of receiving God had been only in the intellectual sense.

Now he finds himself in the very presence of the living God. The fire in the bush was God welling within the fire and shining out through the fire. Now he experiences God personally. God becomes vital and living.

This incident brings to our minds the fact that there are two kinds of knowledge. There is a knowledge that comes from description. One person describes a thing to another, and the other person gains some knowledge of it. We can give knowledge to others by description.

Then there is the knowledge that comes from experience. It is possible to describe a battle fought in a war. But the soldier who has gone through the hell of actual shot and shell and fire knows the battle by personal experience. The memory is for a lifetime. It is something he cannot escape.

It was in this sense that Moses met God at the burning bush. He was a man experiencing the presence of God. To Moses, God was no longer an idea from history but a living Person willing to become involved with His creation, mankind.

There are lessons for us in Moses' encounter with God at the bush in the wilderness.

Why did the Almighty God use a scrubby bush to reveal His presence and glory? It would seem that the bush was just a common acacia plant. It had no intrinsic worth. It was in itself completely helpless. And it could not back out. It was caught there, indwelt by the presence of God and fire.

Like the bush, we will never know God until we are helpless in His hands. We will never be of worth to Him until there is no escape. As long as we can run, as long as we know we can depend upon our avenues of escape, we are not really in God's hands.

Much of our trust in God depends on the fact that things have never gone wrong for us. The crisis time has never come. We figure that God is out there somewhere in case we come to that place of "last resort."

Let me tell you with assurance that the happy Christian is the one who has been caught—captured by the Lord. He or she no longer wants to escape or go back. The happy Christian has met the Lord personally and found Him an all-sufficient Savior and Lord. He or she has burned all the bridges in every direction.

Some of God's children are dabbling with surrender and victory. They have never reached that place of spiritual commitment which is final and complete and satisfying. They still retain their escape routes.

I have come to a sad conclusion about some of the professing Christians around us today. They are poor examples of what Christ is trying to do in our world because they have never willingly given up their doors of retreat. They can get out any time they want to. They can appear to be walking with the Lord as long as things are normal. But when the

tight spot comes, the time of crisis, they opt out.
They want the human solution.

I thank God for the little bush! It was caught, it
was helpless. But it was radiant and useful and en-
during in the presence and hands of the living God.

The other lesson is this: the bush was purified in
the fire.

As a farm boy, I was aware of all those "free
boarders" that attached themselves to the leaves
and the life of the average bush. I knew about the
bugs, the worms, the larva forms, the fungus
spores. They were always there.

But turn a fire loose in the bush for five minutes
and all of the "free boarders" would be consumed.
No germs or microbes or fungus growths remained
after the fire.

God Himself is the holiness and the purity we
need. Some people think of holiness as something
they have for a time, but suddenly God allows them
to lose it. Holiness in the Christian life is nothing
else but the Spirit of God dwelling, filling, satisfying the surrendered, committed, trusting believer.

When will we admit and confess that holiness
comes with the presence of God? When will we believe that a true encounter with God brings purity of
heart?

Christ is not just our Sanctifier. He is our sanctification. He Himself is our holiness. If Christ lives
within our hearts, then just as the fire dwelt within
the burning bush in living encounter and experience, so we will be cleansed and pure. How could it
be otherwise if Christ who is holy and pure lives out
His life in us?

Think also about the blessedness and the security

of that desert bush. Nothing harmful could come to it while it was filled with the presence of God.

There was not a goat anywhere in that part of the world that would have dared approach the bush. The buzzard circling overhead would have been quickly singed by its flame.

If the bush had been burning in that way in our day, do you know what we would do? We would advertise a great Bible conference. We would spend tens of thousands of dollars promoting an international "retreat." We would eat up all the ham and sweet potatoes in the area while we talked and gossiped. Then we would pass a resolution to build a fence around the area containing that miraculous desert bush.

Friend, our preservation and our security do not depend on bylaws and regulations. Our security lies in the presence of God in the midst of His people.

It takes the church a long time to learn some of these lessons. Centuries ago, a serious-minded monk named Simeon Stylites climbed to the top of a pillar 60 feet high and stayed there for 30 years. He said it was his way of trying to preserve his holiness.

My comment is this: If Simeon Stylites had read the third chapter of Exodus, he would have learned that when the fire of God dwells within a person, he does not have to climb 60 feet and be completely without elevator service to be in spiritual safety.

Many years after Moses encountered the personal presence of God in the burning bush, he prayed a wonderful prayer. He said, "Let the beauty of the Lord our God be upon us" (Psalm 90:17).

The beauty of our Lord was in that bush and in

the fire. When Moses saw that beautiful blaze at twilight in the wilderness, he said, "I will now turn aside, and see this great sight." I heard of a Christian woman who was teaching this episode to her Sunday school class.

"We gather from his reaction that Moses had a scientific bent," she said. "Moses turned aside to do scientific research."

Oh, no! Moses was not a scientist. It was the attraction of the presence of God that turned Moses around. And I assure you that it is the beauty and the attractiveness of the presence of God that still turns people around.

After my conversion at age 17, I traveled in fundamental Christian circles. I yearned earnestly for godliness for my own life and for those around me. I had a great desire to be in fellowship with those who were saintly.

I confess that I found much theology but little saintliness! I confess also, at this later date, that I do not care what denomination or group my brothers and sisters in Christ come from if the saintliness of God by the presence of His Holy Spirit is upon them. If Jesus is being glorified in their spiritual lives and service, my heart that still yearns for godly fellowship is attracted to them.

I thank God for every remembrance of simple, godly men and women throughout my ministry. They prayed earnestly, putting their faces up to God, their eyes closed in sacred reverence, until I felt I could see a beautiful light from heaven shining on their countenances.

We need this. How we need this!

Oh, for the sense of sacredness, reverence and

delight in the person and the work of our Savior! It is this more than any other thing that brings beauty to life.

It was a lesson Moses learned. I could wish that every young person going into the Christian ministry could learn it. I could wish that every Christian might learn it!

Christian believers are called to be burning bushes. They are not necessarily called to be great, or to be promoters and organizers. But they are called to be people in whom the beautifying fire of God dwells, people who have met God in the purifying crisis of encounter!

8

"The Treasures of Egypt"

Moses made God his choice, and so should we

WHEN GOD BEGAN TO deal personally with Moses, Israel as a nation had been in Egypt 400 years. The Hebrews were crushed in spirit under their slavery. They were exposed to the idolatry that marked the lives of their masters.

Before God could do anything for His chosen people, He had to demonstrate to them the kind of God He was and is. A discouraged people in subjection and slavery, the Israelites had lost touch with their forefathers' high concept of God and His eternal attributes.

Israel was not expecting very much from God. In their discouragement and ignorance, the people had come to hold too low a view of God, His person and His power.

I have said it before and I will say it again: This low concept of God is our spiritual problem today. Mankind has succeeded quite well in reducing God to a pitiful nothing!

The God of the modern context is no God at all.

He is simply a glorified chairman of the board, a kind of big businessman dealing in souls. The God portrayed in much of our church life today commands very little respect.

We must get back to the Bible and to the ministration of God's Spirit to regain a high and holy concept of God. Oh, this awesome, terrible God, the dread of Isaac! This God who made Isaiah cry out, "I am undone!" This God who drove Daniel to his knees in honor and respect.

To know the Creator and the God of all the universe is to revere Him. It is to bow down before Him in wonder and awesome fear.

God wants to be an experience to us. We need to sense the possibility of being caught between the upper and lower millstones, knowing we can be ground to powder before Him. We need to know what it is to rise in humility out of our grief and nothingness, to know God in Jesus Christ forever and ever, to glorify Him and enjoy Him while the ages roll on.

In Exodus 19 we have the record of Moses' bringing the people of Israel to the wilderness of Sinai. There they camped at the foot of the mount. When Moses ascended Sinai, the Lord said to him, "Lo, I come unto thee in a thick cloud."

The Lord descended to the mount in fire until the whole of Sinai quaked. There was thunder and there was smoke. There was the long, compelling sound of the heavenly trumpet. There was the voice of the Lord.

The living God, the God of Abraham, Isaac and Jacob, did not appear that day in the guise of the God of the modern poet or the God of the backslidden preacher. The One who visited Sinai was no timid, frightened Deity who had to beg leave to exist, who had to ask man's permission to run His world.

The God of the Bible is the true God. He inspires reverence and godly fear. He met with Moses on Sinai that He might free Israel from her false concepts of Himself.

The Israelites in captivity were used to seeing the Egyptians worshiping the sun, worshiping the bull, ram, crocodile, beetle and carp. Egypt had a great variety of everyday gods.

At Sinai God the Creator and Sustainer wanted to give Israel a vision of who He really was. It was as if He was saying, "You must give up all these low ideas of what I am like. Here on this mount I will show you the kind of God I am!" The Lord would reveal His lofty, moral grandeur and His awesome holiness in order that Israel might have a fresh, proper start.

And after all the intervening centuries, God would still reveal Himself to us in the same manner. Why is it we no longer find any sorrow, any tears of repentance in our church life? It is because we do not get the right start as Christians. We do not begin with a vision of the awesome God.

We do not start right because we are jockeyed, cajoled, coaxed, kidded and sometimes pushed into the kingdom of God. We do not have tears because we do not have true repentance. We do not have a higher spirituality because we did not begin right.

We try to convert people by talking them into "accepting Jesus." Then we tell them to join the church, and we get them busy working. All of this is without any proper foundation for faith and discipleship. Too often the foundation is sand, not the bedrock the Bible calls for.

Throughout church history, the great Christians were those who were willing to go down in humility before God. Then they let God raise them up. In our day very few of us are willing to go down.

But back to Sinai, and to Moses and Israel as they met God. Consider the reason for the symbolic representations: the cloud, the fire, the thunder, the sound of the trumpet and the awful Voice.

The cloud speaks of obscurity. We know very well that the human mind cannot comprehend or encompass the person of God. We can know what God is not, but in this earthly life it is impossible for us to say, "I know what God is." We never can know because God belongs to a realm entirely different from ours. The great God exists in awesome wonder. He is uncreated holiness, high above all the things that the hands of mankind have made.

In the Body of Christ, His Church, it is well for us that we should bow our heads and say of Him, "Holy, Holy, Holy, Lord God Almighty!"

Second, the thunder and the lightning were emblems of God's power. A true encounter with God stuns the mind with the sense of God's power. We may think there is great power in the roaring cataract or the erupting volcano, but David once commented, "Power belongeth unto God" (Psalm 62:11).

Power is not something that is an attribute of God. God Himself *is* power. Any human force that we consider power is nothing in God's sight. Consider the great galaxies that blaze throughout the universe. Consider our own sun, moon and planets. Consider the mysteries locked in the atoms. These are demonstrations of God's power. The great God who created all this would bring the human mind to its senses and man to his knees.

The demonstrations of power and the grandeur at Sinai were in essence the desire of God to give Israel a fresh, proper start. God desired Israel, on the eve of her long march through the centuries, to have a high concept of Himself.

There is neither preacher nor teacher anywhere in the world who can say, "Let me tell you all about God!" God told Moses and Israel, and He tells us, "Always there will be the cloud about Me. Always there will be a veil covering My person. While you are on My earth, you will sense this obscurity, for I Am who I Am!"

All of our Christian church denominations that have had great ministries for Christ began with the recognition of God's greatness. God's might and His wise sovereignty were the bedrock upon which their effective Christian witness was founded. Humbled by that concept, they became great.

And I can say this from personal experience: After you have known God and walked with Him by faith for 50 years, growing daily in His grace and the knowledge of Him, you will still see a cloud on Mount Sinai. You will still sense the obscurity. Your mind and your spirit will still bow before Him. Your day of full comprehension is yet to come.

Innate within us is the need to kneel in reverence before something. When God appears to us, and, stunned and overcome, we are bumped to our knees, we have a right start in the life of the Spirit!

Regrettably, that is not the way we are starting men and women in their spiritual journey today. We seem to have reached the conclusion that we can compromise the Christian gospel to make it fit the carnal, unblessed ideas of men.

Compromise is the reason why many churches have become gathering places for buzzards. That is not a graceful way to say it, but it is my feeling.

Do we have to be reminded that Jesus Christ is not on trial before us? But certainly we are on trial before Him.

The record is clear concerning Moses: God spoke to Moses and Moses answered. God was conversing with a man!

Now, why did God single out Moses and perform His will through him? The answer is plain. By his own choice, Moses was God's man. Moses chose to be God's man. God had made His choice first, but Moses agreed to it. Moses made his decision to be God's man, God's servant, God's friend.

Moses had forsaken the luxurious courts of the Pharaohs in Egypt. He had put himself in the way of an encounter with God. He deliberately had chosen spiritual treasures from the hand of God above anything this world could offer.

I know that we live in an era when believing disciples of the lowly, humble Nazarene have more of this world's goods and comforts than any other generation in history. These things conspire to make this a dangerous time for God's people.

Do we know how to receive all of these blessings? Do we know how to be thankful for them and still put God's spiritual blessings and favor ahead of material treasures?

Moses turned his back on the pleasures and treasures of Egypt. Would we, could we turn our backs
on the cash, the comforts, the conveniences we
have in order to be the people of God?

Our Lord knows us very well. Yet He has given us
the power of choice. I believe our Lord Jesus, by the
Spirit of God, keeps whispering to us, "Watch out!
It is very easy to put today's world first and spiritual
treasures second—or last!"

We must make our choice in response. What will
it be?

I confess that I feel a compulsion to cry out in
prayer: "My Lord, I have so many earthly treasures! I must continually give thanks to Thee, my
God, for Thy blessings. But I know that I am going
to have to leave these things, to give them all up
some day. Therefore, I do deliberately choose to earnestly seek spiritual treasures, putting them above
all else. They are the only treasures that will not perish."

Material comfort cannot insure us against spiritual
crises. This world's goods do not preclude the necessity for spiritual choices or growth in grace and
the knowledge of our Lord Jesus Christ. I am positive that God is always pressing us for the better
choices. He would have us continue to decide for
Himself and His kingdom.

Let me try to explain what I mean.

Years ago we had in our church a beautiful Christian who dearly loved the Lord. Jeannie was the
wife of a man employed in the postal service. He,
too, was a Christian and he came to church with
Jeannie, but his mind was always on other things.

I am sure Jeannie prayed much for her husband—

by then a middle-aged man—concerning the choices
he ought to be making. Many others prayed as well.

One day Jeannie's husband asked if he could see
me and talk with me alone. The interview was arranged.

"Mr. Tozer," he began, "I have made up my
mind!"

"You appear to have made a decision about something," I responded to the obvious. "Tell me about
it."

"Mr. Tozer," he continued, "I have been fooling
around long enough. I have made up my mind that
my Christian life will be different. My habits and my
service are going to change!

"You know that I have been a Christian, but I
have just been toying. Many things should be different. I have decided to put myself in the way of
God and His grace. The Lord is going to find me
submissive to His will and obedient to His Word. I
am willing to be a witnessing Christian, and I am
going to start now!"

I hope you are interested in what happened. That
man had made up his mind—and God helped him
mightily. He became one of the very faithful stal-
warts among the men of that church.

By temperament he was quiet and reserved, but
he set up a schedule of testifying for Jesus from
house to house. If a prayer meeting was announced, he would be there. Bad weather never
kept him from church. He began taking his vaca-
tions only when he knew others would be on hand
to carry on the Lord's work.

God is looking for some of us to be different. He is

looking for some of us, like Moses, to forsake the treasures of Egypt.

We need to come to the place of choice. We need to make up our minds, saying and praying, "Lord, take me and use me. I am tired of toying with Thy affections. I am choosing Thy spiritual treasures above everything else!"

Pray that prayer sincerely and you will be brought into a place of blessing that is beautiful, elevated, rich, fruitful and satisfying. It is God's plan that we be shaken loose from our selfishness and earthiness. He longs that we deliberately choose to be His man, His woman.

"I Stand before God"

Elijah knew the way down is also the way up

THERE ARE PEOPLE IN our churches today who think they are being persecuted for their profession of faith in Jesus Christ. I have a word of encouragement and perspective for them.

Take a long look at Elijah the prophet!

They need to ask God to show them the depths of Elijah's courageous faith in God. They need to comprehend the risks he took in one of history's worst times. None of us in our day has been the subject of an evil king like Ahab and a thoroughly heartless, vulgar queen like Jezebel seeking to destroy us. It was an era of intense religious persecution and ungodly vilification.

Elijah faced all of that when he dared to stand for Israel's God. He challenged pagan idolatry and lewd forms of worship. He called the nation back to faith in the God who created it and who sustains the universe.

In any assessment of Elijah, it is necessary to realize the royal odds that were against him as he stood up against Ahab and Jezebel. Yet Elijah dared to remind this couple that they were no match for the

wisdom and will of Jehovah. Jehovah was the great
I AM who had revealed Himself and made a covenant with Israel, His chosen people.

As a prophet in evil times, Elijah had reason to
lean hard on his God. He had come often into the
presence of Jehovah. His is one of the great examples of people born of the seed of Adam, yet willing
and able to press into a deep knowledge of God
through personal encounter with Him.

Like his distant forebear Jacob, Elijah acquired
many spiritual wounds in his militantly prophetic
ministries. Elijah, with courageous faith, took his
campaigns for the glory of God into the very throne
room of kings. Without regard for his own safety
and comfort, he willingly hazarded his life in his
stand against the Lord's enemies.

In the natural and human sense, Elijah had almost nothing to commend him. He dressed in the
rough garments of the Gileadites. He had no background of education or culture. He is first men-
tioned as appearing about halfway through the
reign of Ahab of the Northern Kingdom.

King Ahab had taken as his queen Jezebel, daughter of the King of Sidon. Jezebel had installed
throughout Israel hundreds of priests of Baal, the
chief deity of the Phoenicians. Orthodox priests and
prophets in Israel who protested the pagan idolatry
were silenced or driven out.

Ahab, dominated as he was by Jezebel, gave no
positive, godly leadership in Israel's religious life.
He is condemned in the Scriptures as the most
wicked of the Hebrew kings.

Permit me to speculate a moment concerning bad
King Ahab and his monstrously evil queen, Jezebel.

Did Elijah have instructions from God to write those two off as completely hopeless without any chance of change? We are not God, and we do not know the answer to that question. We do know, however, that salvation is of the Lord. For a man or woman to be saved, there must be an impartation of divine life from above.

We do not come to love God by a sudden, emotional visitation. God would never have asked Ahab and Jezebel to take up a human course of reformation. Love for God and service for God result from repentance, a genuine turning away from the old life and a fixed determination to love God.

Human nature, as we know it, is in a formative state. It is being changed into the image of the thing it loves. It is sad but true that men and women are being molded daily by their affinities. They are being shaped by their affections. They are being powerfully transformed by those things most dear to them. I most assuredly believe that.

We must face the truth that in the unregenerate world of Adam, this power of our affections produces tragedies of cosmic proportions. Was Jezebel always the "cursed woman" whose head and hands the very dogs, with poetic justice, refused to eat? No.

Once she dreamed her pure girlish dreams and blushed at the thoughts of womanly love. But soon she became interested in, and devoted to, evil things. She admired them and at last loved them. There the law of moral affinity took over. Jezebel, like clay in the hands of the potter, was turned into the deformed and hateful thing the attendants finally threw down from the palace window to her death below.

The record in First Kings 17 is terse and concise. Suddenly Elijah, this rough, back-country prophet, is confronting King Ahab in his palace, apparently with no advance notice and without invitation. The foundation of everything that made Elijah who he was is found in his opening testimony to the astonished king.

"As the Lord God of Israel liveth, before whom I stand," he declared, "there shall not be dew nor rain these years, but according to my word."

There is no indication that the surprised king had a chance to say anything before the prophet had turned and was gone. Certainly Elijah had no reason to overstay. In those days of kings' absolute power, if someone out of favor stayed a little too long, it was his head.

Where did Elijah get the kind of boldness that took him to Ahab's throne room to speak for God? The answer comes as no surprise. Elijah may have been lacking in culture and social amenities, but in seeking God for himself, he had found the ultimate Reality.

In finding and knowing and loving God, Elijah had discovered the reality that is permanent, eternal.

Most of us do not see very much of permanence around us in our world. Some while ago, I was given a new definition for *permanent*. I picked up a flyer being distributed in my neighborhood advertising the opening of a new beauty shop. They were offering women a permanent wave, guaranteed to last three months!

So "permanent" is now something that will be around for three months—and we are men and women created by the Almighty God with eternity in our hearts!

The designers and builders who turn out so many of our products with a "planned obsolescence" do not want to talk about permanence. And our "throw away" society seems satisfied to have it that way.

"Seems satisfied," I say. And yet I must admit that mankind evidences a longing for the permanence of the Divine reality. Unfortunately, man's sin and selfishness and scheming stand always in the way. Without God, men and women are unendingly striving—but never finding. They miss the answer pointed out by the hymn writer who said,

Now rest, my long-divided heart;
Fixed on this blessed center, rest.

Too many Christians sing that hymn and others with little thought of the words. If they were honest, they would stop and ask, "What does that really mean?"

The poet was trying to say something significant about God, who wants to become the center of our being. Some of the church fathers talked about "the ground of the soul"—something hidden deep within our beings. It is the ground, the foundation.

Elijah had found that ultimate reality in his friendship with God. He had found something that would never pass away. The average person does not know and probably does not care about this kind of reality, this anchor of the soul. But for Elijah, it was absolute—something beyond and yet something in the midst of the relative.

We have almost made a crisis word out of *relativity*. But I insist there is One who cares for us and knows us. He is not relative to anything except to what and to whom He sovereignly desires to be. That One is God, the living God. Whether men like it or not, He is the absolute!

I have been around long enough and preached often enough to have been called some interesting names. For instance, I have been called an absolutist.

My response? Of course I am an absolutist, and so is every other believer if he or she is worth anything to God and to His testimony. None of us should be scared or offended if we are called absolutists. We must never let words bother us.

Of course we believe in something absolute. Of course we believe in something permanent. We believe in God, the fixed Absolute, to whom we pray, "Our Father, who art in heaven." He it is who tells us, "Come out from among them, and be ye separate, . . . and touch not the unclean thing; and I will receive you, and will be a Father unto you, and ye shall be my sons and daughters" (2 Corinthians 6:17-18).

Do not attempt to argue Elijah out of his faith. He had found the absolute, the ultimate reality. He had found the holy in the midst of the unholy. He had found the Perfect One in the midst of the imperfect. He had found the Infinite beyond the limitations of the finite. He had found the eternal in the temporal.

Elijah had gone far beyond philosophy and its uncertainties. He had found God! It was not a religious theory that Elijah had found. He had found the very key to life and eternity.

God the Creator made us for Himself. Our hearts and beings will never be satisfied until we find our satisfaction in God Himself. Long before Elijah stood in Ahab's presence, Elijah had met God. That was what made his salutation to Ahab so significant: "I stand before God. God is here with me. I stand really in His presence, not yours."

Everything Elijah believed in and stood for had been tested in the fires of experience. We see him standing before Ahab, and the Bible verse comes to mind: "The Word was made flesh, and dwelt among us." God surely gave us Elijah that we might see a man who was the incarnation of what he believed. It is the work of God to make the Word flesh over and over again whenever men or women are born again of the Spirit.

Let me explain. There is a primary sense in which the Incarnation can never be repeated. Only once in the fullness of time could the second Person of the Trinity, the eternal Son, be born of the virgin Mary. The coming of Christ into our humanity stands in lonely grandeur as the mightiest act God ever wrought in all the ages.

But there is a limited sense in which God's Word becomes flesh whenever a lost sinner comes to Jesus Christ in believing faith. In this sense God wants to incarnate the Word in surrendered human lives.

Elijah was constantly learning new lessons of God and His ways with men. That learning continued even after his own human nerves were shattered and his reserves spent as Ahab and Jezebel chased him into the wilderness.

We can learn important lessons by considering God's disciplines in dealing with Elijah. As Elijah fled to the wilderness following his first confrontation with King Ahab, God said to him, "Elijah, go to the brook Cherith, and I will feed you there." God sent big, black buzzards—ravens, scavenger birds—each morning and evening with Elijah's meals. What humiliation! All his life Elijah had been self-sufficient. Now he waited on scavenger birds to deliver him his daily bread.

God also had said, "Elijah, you will drink from the brook." But Elijah had promised Ahab a drought, and his prophecy was true to God's word to him. Elijah was caught by his own cue card. The brook dried up.

Elijah was like so many faithful preachers of the Word who are too true and too uncompromising for their congregations.

"We don't have to take that," the people protest. And they stop contributing to the church. More than one pastor knows the meaning of economic strangulation. Preach the truth, and the brook dries up! But the Lord knows how to deal with each of us in our humiliations. He takes us from truth to truth.

When the brook dried up and there was no rain, God instructed Elijah to go to Zarephath, where he would be fed by a poor widow. We would consider this to be humiliation compounded. It was bad enough to preach the brook dry and to be fed by ravens. But now God says, "There is something else for you to learn, Elijah. A poor widow woman will feed you. But first you must ask her for food."

Well, Elijah obeyed, and we all know the story of the small container of oil and the handful of meal that never ran out. At God's direction, the widow, her son and the prophet Elijah lived for a long, long while on a daily miracle.

How could these things happen? Because a strong, blustery man of faith was willing to be humbled into the dust.

What key do we discover as God faithfully deals with His prophet? It is in James 5:17-18: "Elias [Elijah] was a man subject to like passions as we are, and he prayed earnestly that it might not rain: and it rained not on the earth by the space of three years and six months. And he prayed again, and the heaven gave rain, and the earth brought forth her fruit."

The Lord heard the voice of Elijah because Elijah had been waiting on God to hear the voice of the Lord!

Elijah still stands as one of the great men of God. It is as if God is saying to us, "There is My man, Elijah. He was so great in faith and godliness that when I wanted him up here with Me, I sent a chariot of fire and took him up in a whirlwind!"

But in concluding, let us think of loneliness and trouble and self-pity and discouragement. Do these things ever come with an overwhelming force against God's men and God's women?

Loneliness got to Elijah. He felt that he was the only person on earth who still served the Lord. He felt that he finally was one man against the world. Elijah found out something that we are not teaching very well to new Christians. We ought to tell them that when they follow Jesus all the way, His enemies will be their enemies. We ought to tell them that they will be rejected in this world, just as Elijah—and Jesus—were rejected.

We are getting our new converts off to a bad start. We tell them that following Jesus as Lord is just the smoothest, easiest, slickest thing in the world. "Jesus is not going to lay any burdens on you," we reassure them. "Jesus is going to get you out of all your troubles."

I will come right out and say it: We ought not to tell them such lies!

We ought to tell them that if they will follow on to love and obey the Lord, this world will think the same of them that it thought of Him. What the world thought of Jesus was cruelly demonstrated on a rugged cross atop a hill outside Jerusalem.

Elijah's God still lives. Elijah's walk with God has afforded spiritual inspiration to millions. Look at him and find the secret of humility. Study his life and learn how you can glorify God while you live.

I am a better person because of Elijah. Are you?

10

"I Have Seen Another World"

Isaiah lifts his eyes to gaze on the King of Kings

THROUGHOUT THE LONG centuries of God's dealings with humankind, He has been pleased to give His prophets an almost endless variety of spiritual experiences.

At an important time in the life of Isaiah, God gave him the unusual privilege of gazing through an open window into a heavenly world still invisible to everyone around him.

God had planned a great task and a vital ministry for Isaiah. But as a young man involved in the court life of a successful king, he seemed satisfied with this world and with things as they were. We can say that Isaiah's attention was too strongly focused on King Uzziah.

How was the Lord going to get Isaiah's attention and show him the importance of the world to come? The same way He so frequently does it. He removed the object of Isaiah's interest.

Suddenly, Uzziah, the great and successful king, was gone, taken by death. Isaiah must have been deeply affected, not only as he thought of his own life and career, but as he pondered what Uzziah's passing would mean for the nation of Israel.

I suspect Isaiah stood in tearless grief and looked down at the face of the lifeless king. The silent mouth would issue no more decrees. The royal eyes would never again stare terror into any of his subjects. The royal hand and sceptre would never again be raised in command. The royal head, cold and pale and quiet, no longer wore a crown.

In the human family, that is the way it is, finally. King Uzziah was just another lifeless man, his body a piece of clay about to return to the dust of the earth. Lay the dead body of a king alongside the dead body of a potato grower, and a stranger who has not known either one cannot tell them apart.

The young Isaiah was beyond consolation.

The next thing Isaiah did, however, was the wisest thing he could have done. He raised his eyes from viewing the face of the dead king, and suddenly the Lord enabled him to fasten his gaze upon the eternal King of Kings! Isaiah testified that he saw the Lord sitting upon a throne. He saw God's glory filling the Temple. He saw the seraphim, those created heavenly beings, worshiping God.

He heard the adoring ascription of praise around the heavenly throne: "Holy, holy, holy, is the Lord of hosts: the whole earth is full of His glory."

This other-worldly scene upon which Isaiah was permitted to look raises a question that we do not ask often enough. What has God been trying to say to the inhabitants of our world throughout the centuries past?

In the introduction to his letter, the writer of Hebrews tells us plainly: "God, who at sundry times and in divers manners spake in time past unto the fathers by the prophets, hath in these last days spoken unto us by his Son, whom he hath appointed heir of all things" (Hebrews 1:1-2). In other words, God has revealed Himself many times and in many ways to assure men and women made in His image that there is another and a better world than this vale of tears we refer to as home.

In chapter 11 of that same letter we learn that Abraham, a man of faith and a friend of God, was able to endure throughout his earthly life because he kept his vision and his desires on the invisible things of God.

By now you surely know that I believe there is another world. Although it is a spiritual kingdom, the realm of our triune God, I believe it is distinct and real. I have defined that invisible world rather simply for myself and for any who want to know. It is that spiritual realm ruled over by God the King, into which believing men and women enter by the new birth.

I have no doubts about this. I know what God has promised and I know what I believe. Let the dispensational experts object all they want to. It happens. You simplify something God has revealed, and immediately some theological lint-picker tries to tell you how wrong you are.

Let the Bible experts split it up however they will, let them divide and subdivide it, then tack on a couple of Greek verbs. But when they are through, I will still believe that the kingdom of God is the realm of the Holy Spirit into which men and women enter when they are born from above.

Yes, that invisible world that God has revealed is more real, more lasting, more eternal than this world we are in now. That is why God has given us the prophets and His revelation in His Word. He wants us to be able to look in on the coming world.

When people around us learn that we are involved in a spiritual kingdom not yet visible, they think we are prime candidates for a mental institution. But this we know: Those same people around us are subject to the cruel tyranny of material and temporal things—things that will decay and pass away. No world dictator ever ruled his cowering subjects with any more fierce and compulsive domination than the material, visible things rule the men and women of this world.

Of all the calamities that have been visited upon this world and its inhabitants, the willing surrender of the human spirit to materialistic values is the worst! We who were made for higher worlds are accepting the ways of this world as the ultimate. That is a tragedy of staggering proportions.

We who were meant to commune with the Creator God, with the angels, archangels and seraphim, have decided instead to settle down here. As well might the eagle leave his lofty domain to scratch in the barnyard with the common hens.

Much of our apathy translates into an unspoken response: "I'm just a human being doing the best I can. I do not really have the time to think about God and eternity very much."

Of course we do not have much time! And we do not think about important things because of our 20th century noise and confusion. The devil does everything possible to keep us busy. As a result, very few of us are ever really alone with God.

We boast that we can do things better, move faster and frazzle the nerves of more people, harming their ears and destroying the blessed solitude more completely than in the old days when the best we could do was to shout across the street!

Very few of us know the secret of bathing our souls in silence. It was a secret our Lord Jesus Christ knew very well. There were times when He had to send the multitudes away so He could retire alone into the silence of the mountainside. There He would turn the God-ward side of His soul toward heaven and for a long time expose Himself to the face of His Father in heaven.

I have said it before. We live in a world that gets noisier and noiser. People seem to be children by nature—they love noise!

I was told of a little girl who came home from a birthday party. "Did you have a good time?" her mother asked. "It was great!" she exulted. "All of us got to laughing and then we started screaming. We had fun!"

In our moral, religious, philosophical lives, as in our social lives, the more immature we are, the noisier we are. We cheer ourselves by screaming, "What a great time we are having!"

My eyes and ears and spirit are aware of the immaturities in the so-called evangelicalism of our time. The more noise we make, the more we advertise, the more bells we jingle, the happier we seem to be. All of the signs of immaturity are among us.

We are seeing a general abhorrence of being alone, of being silent before the Lord. We shrink from allowing our souls to be bathed in the healing silences.

It was the practice of Jesus to spend time alone in prayer and communion with the Father. I have been thinking about the record of Enoch, the ancient patriarch. His family members did not go with him when he took a walk, because when he went for a walk it was to commune with God.

When God touched Abraham and said to him, "Leave Ur, your city, and go to the land I will show you," we can be sure Abraham was not engaged in a sociable party or even a coffee klatsch. Unquestionably he was by himself, cultivating his soul.

Twice Jacob had unusual experiences with heavenly visitors. Each time he was alone, in the silence of nighttime. When Moses knelt in the presence of God at the burning bush, he was alone and silent. In the silence, God spoke to him. So it was with the prophets. I doubt that Isaiah would have had his glimpse into the world beyond if he had not been silent and alone. Many of David's psalms were hymns of loneliness, composed in the silence of solitude.

With that as background, I want to say something which may sound strange because it is not heard often in evangelical circles: *There is such a thing as holding familiar fellowship with the powers of the world to come!*

I am sure I do not know all the meaning of that kind of communion and fellowship. I am not sure I can define the powers of the world to come. But it has been the belief of all religious people, including those we find in the Bible, that there is another world above the one we live in. If it is not above geographically or astronomically, it is above in quality of life. It is the kingdom of God.

We are aware that throughout the Old Testament and in the New Testament as well, wonderful heavenly and angelic creatures walked among the people of God. Angels came to Abraham—three of them. And to Jacob. Strange beings came to Gideon as he was threshing. An angel came to Samson's mother when she was in the field. She dashed home to tell her husband. "Come back with me and see this wonderful man!"

Were these disturbed, unbalanced, insane people? Were they fanatics? No. They were normal, sane people. Their subsequent lives and experiences proved it. But in matters of faith, worship and obedience, they had been in touch with another world, a world largely invisible. They had heard another and more compelling voice. They had seen another-worldly vision and had communed with the powers of the world to come.

Now, you may be expecting a personal word at this point. Let me say that I have never in all my life had a vision. I have never dreamed a dream that amounted to anything. So, I am not a visionary in that sense. It may be that I am not enough of a dreamer. But I believe wholeheartedly that we have all the assurance we need that we are not alone in this world. God has not abandoned this earth.

Yes, I believe that God has His messengers, some of them flaming spirits, who are real even while they are invisible to us. You will recall Jesus' comment when exhorting his hearers not to despise little children: "In heaven their angels do always behold the face of my Father" (Matthew 18:10).

When Jesus was being arrested in the Garden of Gethsemane, He said to Peter: "Thinkest thou that I cannot now pray to my Father, and he shall presently give me more than twelve legions of angels?" (Matthew 26:53). Earlier in Matthew's account of Jesus' life and ministry, after Jesus had fasted and prayed and come through Satan's temptation, the record reads, "Then the devil leaveth him, and, behold, angels came and ministered unto him" (4:11).

When Peter was alone in jail, incarcerated for his Christian testimony, "the angel of the Lord" (Acts 12:7) came to him, tapped him on the shoulder and commanded him, "Arise up quickly." The angel led him out of the prison to freedom and reunion with the other believers.

Or go to the chapters of Revelation and gaze for a while into a wonder world called heaven. Throw back the blinds and look into the throne room and see the living creatures and the elders and the angels.

Is all of this nonsense? Do we give in to those who describe these things as fantasies? Will we shrug off these recorded visitations? With a superior attitude and supercilious smile will we conclude that all these things belong to "the childhood of the race"?

No, no! We dare not yield on the reality of the world to come.

When Jesus our Lord was to enter our world as the God-Man to effect the Father's plan of redemption, He was announced to Mary by the angel Gabriel, magnificently referred to in history as the angel of the annunciation. Angels heralded His birth to the Judean shepherds in the fields near Bethlehem. And when Jesus our Lord died and His body had been laid in Joseph's tomb, angels were present for the triumphant announcement, "He is not here. He is risen!"

If you ask me, "Have you ever seen an angel?" my answer is an honest *no*. But I caution you not to sell short the universal testimony of the holiest saints of the ages. We dare not deny the teachings of God's Word. Another world impinges upon this one.

I would say that the doors swing open both ways. Jacob saw the angels going up and coming down, ascending and descending. They had been with Jacob all the time, and he did not know it.

We need a kind of special benediction upon these thoughts. And I think the apostle Peter provided it in his first letter when he spoke of the soon "appearing of Jesus Christ: whom having not seen, ye love; in whom, though now ye see him not, yet believing, ye rejoice with joy unspeakable and full of glory: receiving the end of your faith, even the salvation of your souls" (1:7-9).

The beloved Christians, the elect brothers and sisters to whom Peter wrote, were God's by sanctification of the Spirit and sprinkling of the blood of Christ. Peter testifies that they were believers in what they had not seen and were not seeing. These and all other true Christian believers have always had to hold their faith in God in contrast to the nearly universally held proverb that "seeing is believing."

Any believing that must depend upon seeing may be a kind of believing. At least, it is a conclusion drawn from a testimony of the senses. But believing that must depend upon seeing is not a true New

Testament faith at all. New Testament faith is the believing of a report about things unseen. That is the difference between real New Testament faith and every other kind of so-called believing!

It is characteristic of the Christian that he believes there is a real world coexisting with this world. It is a world that touches this world, a world that is accessible to this one. Notice those three qualifying words.

First, it is a real world. There is never any contradiction between spirit and reality. The contradiction is between spirit and matter, never between the spiritual and the real.

Second, this real spiritual world coexists with our world. There is not a great vacuum between the two. Light and heat coming from the sun coexist and do not exclude each other. So the physical world God made that we call nature and the spiritual world God made that He calls the heavens are coexisting with one another.

Third, the physical world around us and the invisible spiritual world are accessible one to the other. The gates swing in both directions. God could send His eternal Son from the spiritual world to our physical world. And He could carry the martyr Stephen from the physical world to the heavenly. Our prayers can go up and God's answers can come down.

Here is the crux of the whole matter. In this material world, the Christian believes that none of the things he or she can touch are really worth very much. The Christian endures as seeing the invisible, the spiritual—another world. For him or her, that which has real existence is spirit, not matter. A

Christian believes that and lives in the light of it. It distinguishes him or her forever from all brands of materialism and all kinds of superstition and idolatry.

As Christians, we are those whose faith in the invisible has been corrected, chastened and purified by Divine revelation. It is possible to be a believer in the invisible and not a Christian, but it is not possible to be a Christian and not believe in the invisible!

It was our Lord Jesus Christ Himself who brought life and immortality to light through the gospel. He told us of the real world God has prepared for us. Jesus has been there from eternity, and He gave us this final, reassuring word:

"If it were not so, I would have told you."

CHAPTER

11

"The Heavens Were Opened"

In the worst of times, Ezekiel has a vision of God

THE LIVING GOD, the God who willingly made a covenant with a chosen people, laid a heavy burden of prophetic ministry on Ezekiel. The time: about 600 years before Christ. The place: Babylon, where Ezekiel and many of his countrymen lived in captivity.

Ezekiel had been a young priest in Jerusalem before the Babylonian king, Nebuchadnezzar, beseiged and finally demolished the city. Among the ruins were the Temple and Jerusalem's walls. Almost the entire remaining population of Judah was taken off to Babylon, to live in exile and serve the captors.

I have chosen to look at Ezekiel in this series of studies because he had real and dramatic encounters with God. He had experiences with God that were personal and compelling.

Although of the Hebrew priestly line, Ezekiel was called upon to become God's prophetic voice during the exile. God gave him a specific call and minis-

try. He was to convey God's warnings and threats
for continued unfaithfulness. He was to warn the
surrounding nations as well. Finally, he was given a
vision that promised release to the captives and the
restoration of Jerusalem. The Temple would be re-
built. There would again be the true worship of God
in the land.

For Ezekiel in exile it was the worst of times. He
was surrounded by fellow Hebrews who felt complete hopelessness, discouragement and dejection.
Yet in such a setting, the prophet provides us with a
graphic and personal revelation of God and His
glory.

Ezekiel refers to his personal word from God and
his call to speak for God. With clarity and simplicity
he tells us that there were four factors marking his
encounter with God.

First, "the heavens were opened" (Ezekiel 1:1).
Second, Ezekiel was given visions of God. Third,
the word of the Lord came expressly to him. Fourth,
the hand of the Lord was upon him. It is notable
that Ezekiel could pinpoint exactly the details of his
experience with God, right down to the year, month
and day!

A real and vital experience with the Lord gives us
that gracious, abiding sense of God's being there.
Knowing that, we live and move and have our being in God. And as a result, we consciously experience His presence with us.

In our day of advanced photography, I can gather
this reality of Christian experience into an illustra-
tion. If the photographic film has been properly prepared, the lens of the camera needs to open for only
a fraction of a second. That is all it takes for the light

to accomplish its work. That film can then be developed and converted into prints that will remain clear and sharp for years.

So, when a Saul of Tarsus met the living Christ on the road to Damascus, that brief encounter, completely real, changed the course of his life forever. It printed the face of Christ on Saul's sensitized heart. He often referred to the reality of his experience. Stamped ever after within his being was that picture of Jesus.

Returning to Ezekiel's call and commission, we sense the faithfulness of God even when Ezekiel would have said with his Jewish brothers and sisters, "It is no use! There is no hope. We will die in captivity. God must have stayed behind in Jerusalem!"

That is exactly how they felt. As a captive nation in foreign exile, they mourned and said, "Would you demand of us a song in a strange land?" They had hung their harps on the willow tree. They could not sing the songs of Zion in a foreign land.

Young Ezekiel probably had stronger reason for despondency than some of the other exiles. He had been engaged in duties as a priest in Jerusalem at the time of his capture and deportation. He had been ripped away from his position, his work, his calling in the service of the Temple.

Now he was one captive among many by the river Chebar in Babylon. His memories turned back to Jerusalem—back to the Temple, back to the altar and the sacrifices. He thought again of the psalms they used to chant. They were so meaningful at the time.

Suddenly, the Lord is in touch with Ezekiel!

"The heavens were opened," he later wrote, "and I saw visions of God."

The account continues. "The word of the Lord came expressly unto Ezekiel the priest, the son of Buzi, in the land of the Chaldeans by the river Chebar; and the hand of the Lord was there upon him."

When God needs a person for His service—a good person, an effective person, a humble person—why does He most often turn to a person in deep trouble? Why does He seek out a person deep in the crucible of suffering, a person who is not the jovial, "happy-happy" kind? I can only say that this is the way of God with His human creation.

Ezekiel had been uprooted. He had lost everything that was dear and pleasant to him. He was in rude surroundings. If it had happened in this century, we would say he was being held in a prisoner-of-war camp.

We tend to feel that if a man is going to be called upon to do a great task for God, he should have proper and favorable surroundings. Were we calling Ezekiel to service, we would have installed him in a comfortable room overlooking a pleasant lake and extensive gardens. We would reason that such amenities would get him into a proper mood to serve as God's messenger. Fortunately, God does not need our ideas, our religious know-how.

What passes for Christianity in our day is cheap religion. To listen to the current concepts of Christianity, we would conclude it is little more than bits of beautiful poetry, a man-made bouquet of fragrant flowers, a kindly smile for our neighbor and a couple of good deeds on behalf of a brother or sister. Such is today's Christianity.

When I consider some of the elements now offered in Christendom as acceptable religion, I have to restrain myself lest I speak too disapprovingly. I fear my words would be so strong that I would have to repent of them! God will reprove in His own time. There are some things God does not want us to say even about the devil. Michael, the archangel, knew this. He was content to say to Satan, "The Lord rebuke thee" (Jude 9). In other words, "I will just let God handle you!"

But my point is that Christianity is soft on a number of issues that are dear to us. Ezekiel did not come out of pleasant and favorable circumstances. The light had gone out in his heart. He probably thought that God takes a long time to work out His will.

Does not this same view surface in much of our Christian fellowship? We do not want to take the time to plow and to cultivate. We want the fruit and the harvest right away! We do not want to be engaged in any spiritual battle that takes us into the long night. We want the morning light right now! We do not want to go through the processes of planning and preparation and labor pains. We want the baby this instant!

We do not want the cross. We are more interested in the crown.

The condition is not peculiar to our century. Thomas à Kempis wrote long ago, "The Lord has many lovers of His crown but few lovers of His cross."

Christians all around us are trying every shortcut they can think of to get something for nothing in the kingdom of God. When I warn that the shortcuts will not work, someone predictably flares up, ''Isn't grace something for nothing?''

It depends on what kind of grace we are talking about. I am on good biblical ground when I say that some have talked grace while making a god out of their belly. They have turned the grace of God into lasciviousness. These people do not know what the word *grace* means. Because God offers us His grace does not mean that salvation is not costly. It simply means that God gives to us out of His rich and full goodness although we are unworthy of it.

Ezekiel's prison camp situation should remind us of Pastor Dietrich Bonhoeffer and the German dictator, Hitler. Bonhoeffer, as a man of God and a minister for Christ in Nazi Germany, wrote a book, *The Cost of Discipleship*. He put his calling from God as the first of his priorities. Even though he knew he would die for the gospel, he determined to care for his flock of believers. Hitler's police found Bonhoeffer in his study with the Word of God. They took him away and ultimately put a rope around his neck and hanged him.

Bonhoeffer's book has made its way around the world. In it he pointed out his distinction between ''cheap grace'' and ''costly grace.'' Although God's grace has been given freely to men and women who do not deserve it, Bonhoeffer believed it rightly could be called costly because it costs us everything.

Our fathers in the Christian church knew that distinction. But their poor, degenerate sons and daughters do not seem to know it.

When I preach about the grace of God and the fact that Jesus commanded us to take up our cross and follow Him, people respond, ''Oh, you are preaching legalism!'' They try to dismiss me with a wave of the hand. But I am hard to dismiss! I have been preaching this Word of the grace of God and the cross of Christ too long to be easily waved aside. Those who try to rid themselves of my vision of the Christian life today know very well I will be back tomorrow—and with the same biblical message.

I have never been thrown out of a Christian pulpit. But I have had one or two speaking engagements where I was not invited back. I consider that they paid me the greatest compliment they could pay a man. They knew I would open the same Bible and tell them the same truths the second time around!

Ezekiel had reached a low point. If ever he had been a self-confident man, his self-confidence was all gone. There was nothing left for Ezekiel but the humbling confession that only God could help.

Sometimes I have heard people say a humorous thing, but without intending to be humorous. ''I have done everything I know to do,'' they confess, ''and all I can do now is turn the matter over to God and trust Him.'' The Almighty God is the one whom they should have turned to first. Regrettably, we all are guilty at times of turning to God as a last resort.

My church members sometimes come to me, their pastor, because they are having problems in their spiritual lives. I am bothered when they appear to have retained all of their self-confidence. But I am never bothered when someone comes to me in deep, troubled humility. We cannot be too humble.

I once heard a brother preach on the fact that the church should be without spot or wrinkle. To get the wrinkles out of a sack, he said, you fill it. To get a wrinkle out of a rug, you lay it down and walk on it. God sometimes fills us, the preacher continued, but sometimes He just puts us flat down so that everyone can walk on us!

King David long ago knew something of the latter method. He wrote, "The plowers plowed upon my back: they made long their furrows" (Psalm 129:3). I think David was talking about his enemies. And they must have been wearing hobnail boots!

Ezekiel had just come to this kind of a low-ebbed, humbling experience when God opened the heavens. In effect, God put His hand on him and said, "Now I can use you. I have some words and some plans that I want you to pass on to your countrymen."

I cherish Ezekiel's testimony at this point: "The heavens were opened."

Many church people are now going to the "joy boys" for counsel and advice. I call such ministers "chin-chuckers." They advise you to keep your chin up and to get your negative thinking straightened out. Ezekiel found the good hand of God and the will of God when the heavens finally opened. God had been dealing with him. God had been stripping him down. Finally he was ready for God's light.

These joy boys and chin-chuckers who keep saying all is well have done the kingdom of God more harm than a roomful of heretics. When God is dealing with one of His children, we should let God complete His work and provide His light. But in our day we insist on the easiest way out. We refer our people to the popular books whose theme is how easy it is to live the Christian life.

I believe I reply for our Lord Jesus Christ when I say that it is never a snap to carry a cross. It is never easy to closely follow the Man who was scorned and rejected of men. But there is true joy in living for Jesus. In fact, in a time of great persecution, Peter testified that living for Jesus was "joy unspeakable and full of glory" (1 Peter 1:8).

The joy boys will advise you to trade in your tears and start thinking positively. Christ has promised a coming time when the tears will be gone. But I assure you that a Christianity on this earth without tears is no Christianity at all!

Sometimes preachers get carried away and start sermonizing on the great calamities posed by communism and secularism and materialism. But our greatest calamity is the closed heaven, the silent heaven. God meant for us to be in fellowship with Him. When the heavens are closed, men are left to themselves. They are without God.

Ezekiel and all the rest of God's faithful servants learned something that we must learn. If there is anything worth having, it will have to be something that we get from God Himself. The heavens have been closed since mankind began reasoning God out of our world. What used to be the hand and providence of God is now just natural law.

For Ezekiel, the heavens were opened and he saw the visions of God. We should thank the Lord that Ezekiel was able to answer, "Lord, I have been waiting for you. I am at your service!"

And, finally, I would observe that some religious groups in our day seem to have no imperatives. But in the Christian faith it is imperative that the individual meet God. We are not talking about just the possibility of meeting God. We are not saying just that it would be a good thing to meet God. *Meeting God is imperative!*

Thankfully, the gospel of Christ tells us how to find God, to respond to Him, to love Him. The gospel tells us that there is a door—only one door. Jesus Christ is that door, and through Him we meet God.

The gospel tells us that Christ takes God the Father by one hand and repentant sinners by the other and brings them together. He introduces them, and the sinner is reinstated into the favor and grace of God. At Calvary's cross, at the open tomb and at the heavenly throne lost men and women meet God.

The gospel tells us all that. It tells us the saving truth—Christ died for the just and the unjust that He might bring us to God!

Late in the ministry of Charles Spurgeon in London, he wrote: "I can testify that since my conversion [as a young man], I have never, even for 15 minutes, been without a sense of the presence of God."

Men and women who have met God and have chosen to live for Him have found the heavens opened. They have found the world filled with the presence of God. To them it has been, in Milton's words like "a new sun risen on noonday."

And you. If you have never met God in such an experience, He waits to grant you an encounter with Himself.

12

"When Will Revival Come?"

Revival will come when we know God in living experience

IS IT POSSIBLE that the Christian church is now satisfied to accept God as simply the God of history? Does it feel no need for individuals to meet God in living, personal experience?

We do have God in history and Christ in history. But where is the emphasis on the need for a transforming encounter with the living God who transcends history?

In what I have to say I may not be joined by any ground swell of public opinion, but I have a charge to make against the church. We are not consciously aware of God in our midst. We do not seem to sense the tragedy of having almost completely lost the awareness of His presence.

I do not say that to condemn. I say it with a grieving spirit. I pray that the churches in this day may yet reap the joys and fruits of gracious revival and the deep inward awareness of God's presence.

Revival and blessing come to the church when we stop looking at a picture of God and look at God

Himself. Revival comes when, no longer satisfied just to know about a God in history, we meet the conditions of finding Him in living, personal experience.

Conversely, revival cannot come if we are far removed from God. It cannot come if, instead of hearing His voice, we are content with only an echo.

Put those deficiencies together and you have the reason why we are so dissatisfied and empty. You have the reason why there is so little of vivid, vibrant joy in the things of God.

Do you think Abraham would have accomplished what he did in the realm of faith if he had declined his notable face-to-face encounter with God? What would have been Moses' biography had he not experienced God personally?

Jacob lost his reputation as a deceiver and a supplanter and became Israel, "one who prevails with God," when he encountered God at Peniel. It was then that he could say, "I have seen God face to face, and my life is preserved."

Go to Isaiah 6 and you will find the confession of the great prophet who wrote that book under God's inspiration. It was not until he experienced a dramatic confrontation with the Lord of heaven and earth that he was transformed with reverent awe, humility and cleansing. Only then could he say, "Here am I; send me."

Now, let me remind you that we are not just noting the willingness of an Old Testament Deity to reveal Himself to individuals in a dispensation past. It is a great and tragic mistake when Christians are led to believe that there is an Old Testament God, heavybrowed, stern of heart, always condemning, while God the Son, revealed in the New Testament, is tender-hearted, loving, forgiving.

Both the Old and New Testaments teach that the essence of true faith and true worship is the love of God. We are assured that however He manifests Himself, He is always the same God. It is rank error to suppose that the God of Abraham, Moses, Elijah and Isaiah was not the God who fills the pages of the New Testament. This concept would divide the substance of the Deity, contrary to the Scriptures and contrary to all Christian theology.

I hold fast to the opinion that our God is ever trying to reveal Himself to us. There is no way for us sinful men and women to find our way into God's presence unless He reveals Himself and appears to us.

When I say "unless He appears to us," I do not mean that God is trying to appear to our physical eyesight. Rather, He is trying to appear to the eye of our soul through our inner consciousness. I think you will agree that this is not a new concept for serious-minded believers.

Christians are generally committed to the perception that it is possible to see more clearly with the heart than with the eyes. It is possible to feel more tenderly with the heart—our innermost being—than to feel with the tips of our fingers. Never apologize for your inner eyes! They are the real eyes for discerning the nature of issues most important to God. Your physical eyes can fool you, but the eyes of your inner being will give you true guidance.

The apostle Paul wrote about his experience of being caught up into the third heaven. He told us of his vision—the things he was shown. If he had seen those things with his physical eyes, his eyes would have been burned away!

When we see God with the eyes of our hearts, God is fulfilling His purpose to appear to us. To those who ask how this can be, I answer that He can appear to us because we were made in God's image.

In the Old Testament, the writer of the Proverbs taught that true spiritual knowledge is the result of a visitation of heavenly wisdom. It is a kind of baptism of the Spirit of Truth that comes to God-fearing men. This wisdom always is associated with righteousness and humility. It is never found apart from godliness and true holiness of life.

We need to learn and to declare again the mystery of wisdom from above. Truth consists not merely in correct doctrine but in correct doctrine to which is added the inward enlightenment of the Holy Spirit.

It is apparent that we cannot know God by the logic of reason. Through reason we can only know about God. Through the light of nature, our moral reason may be enlightened, but the deeper mysteries of God remain hidden to us until we have received illumination from above.

John the Baptist gave his questioners a brief sentence that I have called the hope and despair of mankind. He said, "A man can receive nothing, except it be given him from heaven" (John 3:27). He was not referring to men's gifts. He was speaking of spiritual truth. Divine truth is of the nature of the Holy Spirit, and for that reason it can be received only by spiritual revelation.

God made us in His own image. He placed within us a capacity for God-knowledge, a capacity to know spiritual things. When our foreparents, Adam and Eve, sinned, that potential died. Thus, "dead in sin" is a description of that part of our being in which we should be able to know God in conscious awareness.

And what have we done to compensate for the loss? We have been forced to depend upon our minds—the seat of our powers of reason and understanding.

In his New Testament letters, the apostle Paul declares again and again the inability of human reason to discover or comprehend divine truth. In that inability we see human despair.

John the Baptist said, ". . . except it be given him from heaven." We are men and women born into this world, and this is our hope. These words do certainly mean that there is such a thing as a gift of knowing, a gift that comes from heaven. Jesus promised His disciples that the Holy Spirit, the Spirit of truth, would come and teach them all things. He explained Peter's knowledge of His Saviorhood as being a direct revelation from the Father in heaven. In one of Jesus' prayers He said, "I thank thee, O Father, Lord of heaven and earth, because thou hast hid these things from the wise and prudent, and hast revealed them unto babes" (Matthew 11:25).

"Except it be given him from heaven." Much of this has to do with the doctrine of our being made in the image of God. We ought to be very sure of what we believe in this matter.

Every person who is born into the world begins to see God in some ways as soon as he or she is old enough to comprehend. If that person does not repent and experience the renewal of regeneration through the working of the Holy Spirit, he or she is lost and will be lost forever. I believe that with all my heart.

But I also believe that human beings, made in the image of God, continue to keep upon themselves something of that image of deity. It is that residual image that permits God to incarnate Himself in us without incongruity or inconsistency. So it was that the eternal Son, Himself God, could become flesh in Jesus Christ without inconsistency.

That is why I say that when God appears in this sense to a man or a woman, it can be so because we were made in God's image. We have something within us that demands to see God. We have something within us that enables us to see God. When God appears to us, He appears to that which is like Himself.

I thank God that for every one of us there is a meeting place arranged with the God who seeks us. That meeting place is the cross of Jesus, the Savior. God arranged for Calvary so we could meet Him. Christ Himself is the Meeting Place between God and man. It is at the cross we can meet God—if the desire is within our beings.

Desire for God is the key in this arrangement for encounter. Surely the woe of this world is that men and women no longer see God and no longer want to see God.

It was God Himself who sent His Son to die for us. That death enabled our Lord, the Son of Man, to take God the Father with one hand and man with the other and introduce us. Jesus enables us to find God very quickly.

Modern mankind can go everywhere, do everything and be completely curious about the universe. But only a rare person now and then is curious enough to want to know God. Have you ever taken time to get alone and to ponder the gracious mystery of how God sought you and found you? Have you meditated on what constituted the hunger within your being that made it possible for you to accept God's gracious invitation and to say, "Jesus, I come!"?

I have thanked God many times for the sweet, winsome ways of the Holy Spirit in dealing with the heart of this untaught lad when I was only 17. We had a neighbor by the name of Holman. I do not know his first name or initials. He was just Mr. Holman. He lived next door to us. I had heard that he was a Christian. But he had never talked to me about Christ.

Then one day I was walking up the street with this friendly neighbor. Suddenly, he put his hand on my shoulder.

"You know," he said, "I have been wondering about you. I have been wondering if you are a Christian, if you are converted. I just wanted the chance to talk it over with you."

"No, Mr. Holman," I answered, "I am not converted, but I thank you for saying this to me. I am going to give it some serious thought."

A little while later, I stopped on a street corner to hear a man preaching. He quoted Jesus' invitation, "Come unto me," and the sinner's prayer, "Have mercy on me."

Those were the two things—the concerned remarks of our neighbor and the exhortation of the street preacher—that bumped me into the kingdom of God. I have always thanked God for our neighbor's witness that helped stir in me the desire for God's forgiveness and eternal life.

Some Christians set up a quota system for their witnessing. I would hate to think that I was Mr. Holman's quota for the day! Witnessing is a matter in which we need the guidance and concern of God through His Holy Spirit.

We know men and women around us who have not had a personal encounter with God. How do we respond when they thank us for being good neighbors? Do we give them any word that might point them in the direction of the Savior?

Sometimes it takes a very little word to stir an unnoticed desire for God and His truth. God Himself is saying to us, "Speak that word. Let Me have the glory. As partners, we will both rejoice in the transformed lives of those around you who are meeting God in personal encounter!"